Human Rights and Development in Africa

Human Rights and Development in Africa

A Continent on a Journey to Extinction

by

Barongo ba Kafuuzi Ateenyi

Strategic Book Publishing and Rights Co.

Strategic Book Publishing and Rights Co.
12620 FM 1960, Suite A4-507
Houston TX 77065
www.sbpra.com

ISBN: 978-1-62516-822-1

"*Colonialism is a system of rule which assumes the right of one people to impose their will upon another. This must inevitably lead to a situation of dominance and dependency which will systematically subordinate those governed by it to the imported culture in social, economic and political life.*" (Brett, E. A., *Colonialism and Underdevelopment in East Africa: The Politics of Economic Change 1919-1939*, Heinemann, London, 1981: Preface)

Warning!

Please, read this book with maximum soberness. Do not look at the titles or none at all, of the writer; or the colour of his skin; or the size and shape of his body; or yet still, where he comes from. Your primary concern should be the communication you receive from the book.

To my beloved and departed sisters:

*Banura Kafuuzi Abwooli and Nyakaisiki
Kafuuzi Adyeeri; the latter who died for the former.
If this book could spark a love like this, we could well claim
we are at the apex of human rights. For, human rights are
such that 'your freedom ends where mine starts'!*

Front cover picture:

Today on the continent of Africa, and increasingly so, you find mass graves of people fallen especially at the hands of the African state. Often, these are innocent people who either were caught in the continent's pervasive wars and conflicts, or were directly targeted by the state agents.

TABLE OF CONTENTS

ILLUSTRATIONS

FOREWORD

If you were well dressed—decently dressed; if you were confident that you have all your mental capacities about you; if you didn't think that anything was wrong about you; but if you passed some people and they laughed at you; they made fun of you; what would you do?

If you discovered that some people even regard you as non-intelligent, i.e., sub-human; if you reached for a place to sit and those you found moved away in distaste of being seen seated with you; if you felt that people even feel embarrassed to be equated with you; what would you do?

If, due to your skin colour, you were treated like an object in circumstances you cannot possibly fight back; if you indicated that you were distressed about the way those people treated you but they chose to continue like nothing has happened; what would you do?

This is the experience I got when I was in Israel in 1995. However, I must point out that this was not the case in all places I went in the country. In some places, I was treated quite humanly, while in others I was reduced to a simple laughing stalk. So, I wanted to know why things were like this. I had heard that Africans, or 'blacks,' are usually regarded as sub-humans by light-skinned peoples. But I had not gotten the opportunity to experience this—not until I was in Israel.

Again, I must point out that I hold no grudge against anybody for the treatment I was subjected to. Nor do I feel stressed about the experience anymore. Why? Because given their position then and they mine, I might have behaved just the same. For I would not understand why, in the twenty-first century, we, in Africa, still die of jiggers! I would not understand why, for all the years we have been so-called independent, we still import jet fighters, tanks, and other military hardware to kill our very own—I mean, we fight more internal wars within our state systems than we fight against other nations! We fight more civil and ethnic wars than we fight international wars!

I wouldn't understand why we repress and torture our own, and why we die of hunger and starvation in this paradise of plenty! For wasn't it said that our continent is possibly the most endowed on earth, and that this is why the first humanity on earth could have lived on Africa? Then why do we chronically suffer from hunger and starvation?

I would not understand why our resources benefit the foreigners more than they do us! I would not understand why we are chronically plagued by instability! Therefore, I could only laugh at the gross irony—at the unfortunate absurdity! This could be the reason why they laughed then and why they must laugh today.

Barongo ba Kafuuzi Ateenyi
Kampala, April 2010

PREFACE

On a short course—a field study internship programme in Israel in 1995—I was struck by a realisation of the forces that govern human motion. Most importantly, I was fascinated by a discovery that human freedom is perhaps the greatest factor that determines human development.

I had come from Africa on an Israel Government scholarship and, on reaching Israel, I, together with my colleagues on the course, was introduced to the ancient history of the country, including its intermittent occupation and banishment from the land by ancient Egyptians, Persians, Greeks, Romans, and others.

The most recent such occupation and banishment was about two thousand years earlier, the latest return being towards the end of the nineteenth century. However, by 1948 (about seventy years later), Israel had recovered nation and statehood, and declared independence. Nevertheless, going through its history and what I personally witnessed in the country, I came to the conclusion that perhaps there is never a force in nature greater than human intelligence.

At the time, I looked at what the people in Israel had achieved over the years and looked back at my own people in Africa, who—except for a short period of human trafficking (slave trade) of about three hundred years (i.e., from the sixteenth to eighteenth century)—had never, in fact, left their lands, at least *en masse* or been dominated for so long. But we seemed as if we had just started to appear on the surface of the earth!

As Africans, we had almost nothing to show for the time we had lived on earth, yet it is widely believed that we are possibly the oldest human race in the world! We were basically at zero, and the question was: Why should it be like this? Why was there such a gross difference between us and other people in the world? Could it be a biological, i.e. intellectual difference, as some people have argued? This and many other questions bombarded me in a manner that I could not possibly contend with in such a limited time. However, as lack would have it, I had, as part of my course at Rehovot Development Study Centre, to do research at Israel Family Farms (*Moshavim*), where I interacted with the people there and was able to read into their minds.

I discovered that the engine that drives everything in Israel is the phenomenon of human freedom. Except for the insecurity concerns from without the country, the people inside feel so free that they least harbour any fear of a fellow human being. This contrasted drastically with the situation in Africa where people fear their leaders. In Israel, one is a leader only by the office he or she holds. No more! They don't exceed that office. But in Africa, a leader is a leader night and day, Saturday and Sunday—even in people's private homes! In other words, in Africa, leaders own the people instead of the people owning the leaders!

My concern then was why should it be like this in Africa, yet it was different in other places? It took me quite some time to unravel this mystery. However, gradually, I discovered that in Africa we actually don't belong as peoples, but possibly as strange creatures. In other words, we were a people without a human face! That is why we were treated less like animals!

I also discovered that we don't have names of ourselves; instead, we have other people's names. Basically, we don't know who we are. This is to say, we are people without identity! And because we don't know who we are, we can't know what we want in life. And because we can't know what we want in life, we cannot get it. Thus, we cannot achieve development. This is the reason we lagged behind the rest of the world.

Finally, I discovered that the engine to human development is self-seeking and self-invention, i.e., self-discovery. Humanity has to seek itself in order to reinvent itself. But if people don't know who they are, they cannot seek themselves or invent themselves. Thus, they cannot develop. This is another reason why africa lagged behind the rest of the world.

These discoveries were so painful, yet exciting. They were painful because of the realisation that, as a continent, we had lost more than a century of growth and development. But they were exciting, too, because I personally believed I had made a fundamental discovery about africa, perhaps one of the greatest discoveries ever made about a continent. I strongly believed I had found a basis for solving Africa's pervasive development problems. From then on, I was not going to rest until I had found a final cure. This document, therefore, is a product of soul-searching for a whole fifteen years.

The book focuses on the many development challenges afflicting Africa, leading to the continent's dismal social, economic, and political performance in the world today. While it is appreciated that development is a phenomenon of progressive and gradual change and transformation, the question is: Why have these situations eluded Africa for so long?

Africa is the poorest continent in the world; it is said to have thirty-three of the world's forty-eight least-developed countries, and almost half (more than half a billion) of its population is living in extreme poverty. Africa also hosts the most illiterate, most diseased or disease-prone, and most unstable situations on earth. The question then is: Why have these situations remained for so long in Africa?

The book places the problems in contemporary times in order to make them relevant to modern understanding and solutions. The approach is human rights analysis, focusing on the interrelationship between human rights and development in general and particularly on the African continent.

If well understood, the book is expected to save the many years or decades of wars and conflicts that usually characterize the African continent in the name of so-called liberation struggles or revolutions to bring change on the continent. And in so doing, it is expected to save the many human lives and resources that continue to be lost in such struggles. For, all these situations must continue, as they have always done, to come to nothing unless we appreciate the true African problem, which this book endeavors to explain.

Barongo ba Kafuuzi Ateenyi
Kampala, April 2010

ACKNOWLEDGEMENTS

In an environment devoid of institutional charitable interests to support a work like this, my family became my major anchor. And even if I stressed them so much for what they otherwise regarded a non-consequential work with possibly no practical implications, they, nevertheless, bore my resilience with unending patience. I owe it to them; to Kansiime Ateenyi who cooked my food in the book's last days; and I must add, Martin Masiga and Charles Abola who added a hand when the going got rough. Of course, I can't mention everybody who wished me well and helped me on this task. However, I return my sincere wishes to them all.

THE MAIN ARGUMENTS IN THE BOOK

Introduction

This is a study of the undercurrents – the circumstances that determine the motion and dynamism of a society, and the after-effects. It is a study of more than what is usually apparent to our eye.

Theory one

Human rights: Human rights are circumstances or situations that qualify and define humanity as one. They define you and me.

Theory two

Human rights and essence: You are either human, and you have human rights; or you are nothing at all, thus you have no human rights. Therefore, to have human rights is to be human; and to be human is to have human rights.

Theory three

Human rights and freedom: To have human rights is to have freedom – to be free. This should be both at individual and societal level. At individual level, to have freedom is to have human respect, i.e. to be regarded as one. At societal level, to have freedom is to have ability to determine own social fate.

Theory four

Humanity and identity: Humanity has no colour or race or religion. It has no height or weight. In fact, humanity has no limbs (legs, arms or hands) but the human brains. This is the cut-off point that it takes to be human. Note that I'm not saying that colour or race or religion do not exist. I'm only saying they don't matter in as far as defining humanity is concerned. Therefore, to determine humanity by colour or race or religion is to miss the point. In fact, to define humanity by the limbs it has or it has not, is to miss the point too.

Theory five

The Concept of Human Development: Development is defined only in terms of humanity, i.e. in terms of the human individual. That is to say, development is defined as human development. It is the transformation (intellectual) of an individual from one level of social production to another. When I speak of social production, I don't mean production for society but production in society. And when I speak of the human individual, I don't mean one for all, but one in all. In which case, development becomes a social phenomenon, rather than an individual phenomenon.

Theory six

Development and socio-economic transformation: Development is the socio-economic transformation of a society, where socio-economic transformation is the attainment by society of capacity to transform itself from one level of social production to another – usually a higher level.

Theory seven

Development and political transformation: But development is also the political transformation of a society. That is to say, it is the attainment of ideological capacity both in terms of real social organisation and maturity of mind to appreciate what is best for society to attain stability and continuity.

Theory eight

Economic development: Economic development is the attainment of economic wealth, regardless of the means of attaining such wealth. This means that humanity can attain economic development without attaining actual development. This is neither desirable nor sustainable because, as humans, we are producers of economic wealth more than mere consumers of economic wealth. In other words, we should be above this.

Theory nine

Development and human rights: Development is a factor of human rights. Therefore, development is a factor of humanity. That is to say, you are either human; therefore, you are capable of development; or you are nothing at all, thus incapable of development.

Theory ten

Self-invention and Self-recreation: Development is also the attainment of capacity for self-invention and self-recreation. Self-invention and self-recreation is the attainment of capacity to sustain oneself in real life. It is the attainment of self-actualisation, which occurs when one attains capacity to change one's life fundamentally, i.e. when one can live forever.

Theory eleven

Human dynamism: Humanity is constantly changing, i.e. it is either developing or declining. It never stagnates. The maximum of human development is self-sustenance in life; while the maximum of human decline is extinction. Self-sustenance in life is when humanity can live forever, while extinction is the total disappearance of humanity from the surface of the earth.

Theory twelve

Conditions for human development versus those for human extinction: The conditions for human development are the attainment of human rights; but those for human extinction are the lack of human rights. Human development occurs when we enjoy maximum human rights; while human extinction occurs when we lack human rights. Because this leads to loss of capacity to produce for self-sustainability.

Theory thirteen

Forms of human extinction: Human extinction occurs in one of two forms or both; with each naturally leading to the other. Either it occurs in form of loss of intellectual capacity to produce for self-sustainability; or it occurs in form of extreme instability, i.e. in form of incessant wars and strife. But loss of intellectual capacity must naturally lead to extreme instability, and vice versa.

Theory fourteen

Social stability versus social instability: Social stability is the attainment of continuity and sustainability in society; while social instability is the lack of these. Social stability comes about as a result of the attainment in society of the institutions that contribute to social order and continuity; while social instability comes about as a result of the lack of these. Therefore, the presence or lack of these institutions in society is in itself a reflection of social stability or instability respectively.

Theory fifteen

Social institutions: Social institutions are the rules, laws, customs, and habits, formations or practices that ensure social order. Social institutions, on the other hand, are the norms and standards that sustain stability in society.

Reality one

Africans lack human rights both at individual and societal level. Therefore, Africans lack human freedom both at individual and societal level. This condition hails from the western colonialism of the nineteenth century on the continent, but continues to be perpetuated by the current African state.

Reality two

Africans continue to be ruled from without, though this time by fellow Africans. This is what is called internal colonialism, if looked at from outside the continent.

Reality three

Africans cannot, therefore, develop because they are not free.

Reality four

Since they are not free, and cannot, therefore, develop; this is what explains their condition, i.e. the incessant wars, poverty, disease and general strife and decline on the continent.

Reality five

It is said that Africa hosts thirty-three of forty-eight least-developed countries in the world – with half a billion of its people living in abject poverty. The continent hosts the most illiterate, most diseased or disease-prone, and the most socio-economically and politically unstable situations on earth. We, in effect, occupy the basest of the world's positions.

Reality six

Africa is heading for extinction. What we see on the continent today in form of incessant or even periodical wars and strife; and what we see as increasing illiteracy, poverty, hunger and disease, is but extinction taking place on the continent. This is notwithstanding the alleged rising GDPs and Income per Capitas; or better still, an alleged democratisation trend today on the continent. These are as deceptive as they are fictitious. They are neither founded in the populations, nor are they sustainable.

Reality seven

Africa can only be saved from extinction by a reversal of its current conditions. This is either through a revival of the continent's socio-political order before colonial imposition in the nineteenth century; or a genuine review of the current state on the continent. That is to say, the solution entails a re-awakening of an African social formation as it were before western colonialism; or a free and sincere review of the current state with a view to giving people a chance to choose where to belong. This is what is called independence. Otherwise, short of this, extinction is real.

1

INTRODUCTION

1.1 Background

This book idea was born out of a long-seated personal desire to understand the many development challenges afflicting Africa, and in particular, to appreciate why Africa as a continent lags behind the rest of the world in socio-economic and political development.

Africa is the poorest continent in the world; it is said to have thirty-three of the world's forty-eight least developed countries, and almost half (more than half a billion) of its population is living in abject poverty. The continent also hosts the most illiterate, most disease-prone, and most socio-economically and politically unstable situations on earth. The question to the author then was: Why should Africa be like this?

The author has perceived the continent's problems as the persistent failure of social, economic, and political development, manifesting in persistent dictatorships; economic decline; and rampant political instabilities, often resulting in massive deaths, large population displacements, and attendant effects such as the deepening poverty, disease, hunger, and starvation. He has also sought to contribute solutions to redress the situation.

1.2 Rationale

This book approaches the concept of development from the point of view of human development. In other words, according to the author, development must be defined and indeed practiced in terms of the human individual. This, according to the author, is in contrast to the traditional approach where development is often looked at in terms of economic accumulation regardless of the means of such accumulation and the subject (i.e. the target) of consumption.

1.3 Thrust of the book

This book assesses development from the human perspective, and analyses African development challenges, especially beginning with the alleged independence in the 1960s. In particular, the book examines the trends of growth and development on the African continent, with specific reference to the capacities of the people to sustain themselves in life.

1.4 The theory

The author has argued that there is an inevitable (organic) link between human development and human rights. According to the author, development and human rights underpin each other, but more so, human rights forms the basis (the bedrock) upon which development is founded. According to the author, development without the human face is no development at all.

1.5 The premise

The author argues that there is failure of the understanding and practice of human rights on the African continent, which has given rise to the failure of human development on the continent. According to the author, this failure is by all actors on the continent—state and non-state actors—but state actors are major. The author goes on that the failure has given rise to a phenomenon of human extinction on the continent.

1.6 Objectives

In order to achieve the above, this book seeks to answer six major questions as follows:

a) Why has Africa persistently failed to develop socially and economically despite its vast natural resources?

b) Why is Africa chronically afflicted by social and political instabilities, resulting in massive deaths, large population displacements—both internal and external—and the surging poverty, disease, hunger, and starvation?

c) Why does Africa chronically suffer from political dictatorships?

d) Why is Africa increasingly afflicted by financial and political corruption?

e) What do the above situations imply for Africa?

f) What should be done to address the situations?

1.7 Working Concepts in the Book

1.7.1 Human Rights

Overview

While there have been multiple authors and researchers on human rights, many have tended to approach the concept as given (known) rather than from an articulated point of view.

In other words, they never bother to define it or explain its meaning. This book, however, attempts to define the concept and demonstrate that human rights are perhaps the most important aspect of humanity.

Definition

The concept of human rights is broad, encompassing social, cultural, economic, political, environmental, and religious circumstances that we need as humans in order to live. In other words, human rights are those conditions that make us human. Without them, we are not. Human rights are also prerequisites to our very existence. Without them, we cannot exist as such.

Inalienability of human rights

Human rights are inalienable and non-derogable, which means they cannot be taken away (i.e., alienated) from the individual if that individual must remain as such. This is to say that human rights cannot be reduced in quality or scope without harming the very human individual.

The totality of human rights

Human rights are total. They are the constitution (composition) that makes humanity, and without them humanity is not. Human rights are also complete. In other words, they cannot be divided.

The inherent-ness of human rights

Human rights are also inherent, i.e., we are born with them. We cannot function as human without them. Kofi Annan, former Secretary General of the United Nations (1997-2006) emphasised this in the observation that:

"Human rights are the foundation of human existence and coexistence. They are universal, indivisible, and interdependent. And they lie at the heart of everything the United Nations aspires to achieve in its global mission of peace and development."[1]

According to this view, human rights are central to the very existence of humanity.

According to Donnelly,[2] human rights are the rights that one has simply because one is human. However, Donnelly does not go beyond this flat definition; instead, the author uses the concept as given. But the author observes that this 'deceptively simple idea' has profound social and political consequences, noting:

"Human rights, because they rest on nothing more than being human, are universal, equal, and inalienable. They are held by all human beings, universally. One either is or is not human and thus has or does not have human rights, equally. And one can no more lose these rights than one can stop being a human being..."[3]

According to the author, therefore, one is entitled to human rights and is empowered by them. Suffice then to state that

---

[1] Foreword in: United Nations Office of the High Commissioner for Human Rights (UNOHCHR), *Human Rights: A Compilation of International Instruments*, Vol. 1, First Part, Universal Instruments, New York & Geneva, 2002, p. xiii.

[2] Donnelly, Jack, "What are Human Rights?" in *Introduction to Human Rights*, Clack, et al (Editors), http://usinfo.state.gov.

[3] P. 3

Donnelly's view forms the basic foundation of this book, i.e. human rights are central to human existence.

Conde (2004) has argued that human rights are the birthright of humanity, and their protection is the first responsibility of all states. According to the author, human rights are inherent attributes of the human personality, and their purpose is the legal protection of the inherent dignity of each individual human being. However, while the author's view regarding human rights is appreciable, the author has approached the concept from a legalistic point of view, by especially importing the concept of the state to protect human rights. Yet human rights precede the concept of the state.

According to the current book, human rights existed before the existence of the state. Human rights—since they are human attributes—existed before the creation of the state by humanity. In other words, since human beings existed before the state and society, human rights also precede the state and society. Moreover, human rights also supersede the state.

According to Maddex (2000), human rights are substance to which every person is entitled simply by virtue of being a human being living in a society of other humans. Whereas this author tends to bind the concept of human rights to the concept of society, just like Conde above, the author fails to appreciate the fact that human rights existed before the emergence of society. Human rights are inherent in human nature; therefore, they existed before the creation of society by people.

Nevertheless, Maddex helps to delineate some critical aspects of human rights, such as that they constitute the right to life, liberty, and the security of person.[4] According to the

---

[4]   p. xxviii

author, human rights are the equivalent of human freedom. The author goes further to add that strictly speaking, human rights arise out of the conflict between the goals of an individual in a political system and the goals of those who wield political power in that system.

Nevertheless, it can be seen here that the author's view of human rights reduces to one of being political and dialectic. In other words, it becomes an issue of conflict and competition in the human struggle for resources (economics) and political power (politics). Yet the current author holds the view that if to be human is to have rights, and if to have rights is to be human, then human rights precede society; therefore, human rights precede the state and politics.

Wanyande (1991) has argued that the rights and freedoms—such as the right to life, property ownership, freedom of conscience, freedom of worship, freedom of association or assembly, etc.—are referred to as inalienable because they existed before the founding of governments. According to the author, everybody is born with these rights and freedoms, and individual rulers do not give them, however powerful they may be. According to the author, constitutions or governments do not give or take away human rights, but they only guarantee them.[5] It can be seen here that Wanyande agrees with the current author that human rights precede the state. But, as before, the current author would add that human rights supersede the state. This is why the state must protect them but not take them away.

---

[5] P.1

Benedek (2003) has argued that human rights are universal and inalienable, which means they apply equally everywhere and cannot be taken away from any person, even with his or her agreement.[6] According to the author, human rights are also indivisible and interdependent.[7] It can be seen that this view is in line with the current author's argument that human rights are total. In other words, human rights are comprehensive (i.e., concerning all aspects of humanity—social, cultural, religious, economic, political, environmental, etc.); they are complete (i.e., encompassing all aspects of humanity); and they are supreme (i.e., most important to humanity). Human rights are the material that constitutes humanity.

1.7.2 Development

'In order to determine whether a society is developing, one must go beyond criteria based on indices of per capita income (which, expressed in statistical form, are misleading), as well as those which concentrate on the study of gross income.

---

[6] P. 20

[7] The United Nations Population Fund (UNFPA), defines *indivisibility* of human rights as *'having equal status, and not being able to be positioned in a hierarchical order'*; and *interdependence* as *'each one contributing to the realization of a person's human dignity through the satisfaction of his or her developmental, physical, psychological and spiritual needs'*. The source goes on that 'denial of one right invariably impedes enjoyment of other rights; thus, the right of everyone to an adequate standard of living cannot be compromised at the expense of other rights, such as the right to health or the right to education. Additionally, the source asserts that the fulfilment of one right often depends, wholly or in part, upon the fulfilment of others. Source: United Nations Population Fund (UNFPA) at http://www.unfpa.org/rights/principles.htm.

The basic, elementary criterion is whether or not the society is 'being for itself,' i.e., its political, economic and cultural decision-making power is located within'

—Paul Freire[8]

In this book, development is adopted only as human development, i.e., human progressive change that takes three forms: ideological, scientific-technological, and material or physical transformation. Human development is different from economic development in that economic development is the mere accumulation of wealth or physical property—sometimes regardless of the means or the purpose of such accumulation.

According to Hollnsteiner,[9] human development is when people and their active participation matter. The author goes on to say that through participatory development, the currently marginalized poor become aware of the range of value choices open to them and their social and political implications. However, this theory falls short in that it does not tell us how these choices are fulfilled. Instead, it tells us the role of the people in arriving at, i.e., making those choices. This is, in all aspects, insufficient for the understanding of development.

Writing in 1983, Gram noted that a study of human development in the recent past had demonstrated that the processes that perpetuate relative or absolute poverty for more than a billion people in the Third World, and for many

---

[8]   A cross-quotation from Stan Burkey, *People First: A Guide to Self-Reliant, Participatory Rural Development*, zed Books Ltd., London, 1993.

[9]   Foreword in: Gram Guy, *Development By People: Citizen Construction of a Just World*, Praeger, New York, 1983.

millions elsewhere, are logical products of a world system at work. According to the author, following conventional ideas of economics and politics would not change this reality, and a paradigm shift for all of human development was therefore necessary.[10]

According to Burkey (1993), development in any meaningful sense must begin with and within the individual. The author notes that unless motivation comes from within, efforts to promote change will not be sustainable by that individual. According to the author, the individual will remain under the power of others.[11] According to this theory, therefore, development must be internally derived and driven in society.

Ideological development: Ideological development is the attainment of better skills for social organisation. According to Wikipedia,[12] an ideology is a set of conscious and unconscious ideas that constitute one's goals, expectations, and actions:

> "An ideology is a comprehensive vision, a way of looking at things as in several philosophical tendencies, or a set of ideas proposed by the dominant class of a society to all members of this society."

According to this source, the main purpose behind an ideology is to offer either change in society, or adherence to a set of ideals where conformity already exists, through a normative thought process. According to the source, therefore, ideology is a set of established thought or value

---

[10] Preface.

[11] P. 35

[12] http://en.wikipedia.org/wiki/Ideological

systems by which a society or community may be guided or led, especially by those in power. However, the present author holds that an ideology may be used in or outside society—to guide an individual's actions—especially since ideology is a state of mind. In addition, the author holds that an ideology may be a set of ideas or values for the betterment of society. This means that ideological development is the attainment of better knowledge and ideas for the better organisation of society.

Scientific and technological development: Also termed economic growth, scientific and technological development is the attainment of improved methods of production of goods and services. According to Beardshaw and Palfreman (1993), the changes in industry in the first half of the twentieth century are often referred to as the *Scientific Revolution* because advances in ('for instance') chemicals, electricity, and aeronautics were based upon the application of theoretical sciences such as physics and chemistry to industry[13]. According to the source, these advances were often made by people with little scientific knowledge, a view that the current book builds upon to argue that there is perhaps an inherent impetus in human beings to reinvent themselves.

Brett (1981) adopts a concept of growth that is often used in literature on economic development, which takes development as related primarily to growth in the monetary economy, and therefore to the introduction of modern technology and the expansion of production for the market.[14] While this view takes into account technological change as

---

[13]   P. 19

[14]   P. 16

an aspect of economic growth—as, indeed, adopted by the current author—the current author believes that Brett is inclined more to restricting growth to monetary or market economics. But economic growth has always occurred even before the invention of money and the market concept. Among primitive people, for instance, there was no monetary or market economics. But somehow humanity reinvented itself. This is because, consciously or unconsciously, humanity has always advanced itself.

And when discussing growth and development, Cornforth (1987) asserts that the two are different in that growth is quantitative change in phenomena, while development is qualitative change that does not necessarily involve change in quantity. According to the author, economic growth is the attainment of better methods of production.

Material or physical development: Material or physical development is the qualitative change in the living conditions of people. This is the attainment and enjoyment of improved conditions of living, such as food, shelter, health, water, clothing, knowledge, information, etc. However, if material development must occur, these conditions must derive from within society. Otherwise, it will not be sustainable. For instance, trade and aid alone cannot lead to development unless either can cause technology transfer.

Technology transfer is the transmission and infusion of ideas from one society to another, leading to an equilibrium shift in the technical capacity of the later society. In other words, more than the physical transfer of goods, machinery, moulds, or dummies—which is mere trade; technology transfer is the infusion of techniques (i.e. knowledge and ideas) from one society to another. In this case, development would be sustainable only when founded on these.

1.8 The Link Between Human Rights and Development

Donnelly[15] has argued that one is entitled to human rights, as well as is empowered by them. This is because in the process of self-seeking, the individual advances himself or herself. Stretched further, this means that human rights are fundamental to human development, and development must be the outcome of enjoyment of human rights. Akankwasa (1999) underlines this further when the author observes that people's participation in the development process is fundamental to their realisation of any development. According to the author, human rights are the basis for human development and one way of enjoying them is by popular participation in matters that affect the people.

Preamble 5 of the United Nations Declaration on Social Progress and Development[16] underlines further the above argument by stating that humanity can only achieve complete fulfilment of its aspirations within a just social order. According to the authority, humanity requires a free and safe social, political, and environmental order in order to realise its maximum potential. This underscores the basic argument of the present book: that human rights and development underpin each other.

1.9 Rationale for the Book

The book idea was born out of a long-seated personal desire to appreciate and contribute to solving Africa's many development challenges. The author has looked at Africa's development problems as the persistent failure of socio-

---

[15] Op. cit, p.3
[16] http://www2.ohchr.org/english/law/progress.htm

economic and political development, which manifests in persistent dictatorships; economic decline; and rampant social and political instabilities, resulting in massive deaths, large population displacements—internal and external—and the attendant effects, such as deepening poverty, disease, hunger and starvation. In addition, the author has looked at the worsening political and financial corruption on the continent, and sought to provide recommendations for solutions.

1.10 Methodology

The author has adopted a desk research to assess the continent's development problems, in addition to what he personally knows as an African. The approach is an analysis of the trends on the continent, especially beginning the 1960s when most of the continent's contemporary states purported to have attained independence.

This book also adopts a structural analysis to assess the problems of the continent by closely examining the forms (i.e. patterns) of political organisation on the continent, rather than the content of governments. It is the author's view that Africa's development challenges arise not from the content of governments or regimes, but from the forms or patterns of political organisation on the continent. The author argues that the concern with content is a concern with symptoms rather than with the disease and its causes. Finally, the author has adopted a case study to illustrate the arguments presented in the book.

2

THE PROBLEM:
AFRICA'S DEVELOPMENT CRISIS

"By the end of the nineteenth century, Europe and Africa confronted each other in respective states of development and underdevelopment, the latter term being defined by Europeans in relation to the lack of African progress in the techniques required to sustain an advanced materialistic culture. Whatever one's feelings about the relative philosophical merits of the two styles of life, there is no doubt that the apparatus of Western culture was infinitely superior to that of Africa in subjecting others to its will. Its control over the scientific revolution and its products in the fields of warfare, administration, and economic production enabled it to 'discover' the world beyond its own, to conquer this and divide it up between the leading European nations. In the face of such odds, African opposition was quickly overcome and unequal relations between the two forces were regularised through the creation of the colonial system, which rapidly transformed the undeveloped of African society into the underdeveloped of colonial society." (Brett, E. A., Colonialism and Underdevelopment in East Africa: The Politics of Economic Change 1919-1939, Heinemann, London, 1981: Preface)

15

2.1 Economic Failure and Decline in Africa

Writing on a record of failure in Africa, Harrison (1989) noted that no one who has travelled much in the world can fail to notice how things tend to go wrong in Africa:

> "There is hardly a hotel room without its stock of candles against inevitable power cuts. Projects are paralysed as jeeps are mothballed for months, waiting for spares. Graveyards of immobilised, rusting bulldozers or mechanical shovels are a common wayside spectacle. Communications are unreliable ... Dirt roads compress into ridges like a corrugated tin roof, shaking vehicles gradually to bits. Tyres wear out faster ... Projects, policies and programmes are as breakdown-prone as equipment."[17]

According to the author, major aid agencies like the World Bank and USAID have increasingly come to acknowledge the disastrous performance of aid in Africa.

The above view was echoed by Wanyande,[18] who observed that in addition to being faced with the rapidly deteriorating food situation and increasing dependence on food aid and food imports, Africa continued to face increasing mass poverty, including the risk of natural resources depletion and environmental degradation. According to the author, life expectancy at birth in the continent remained low, while nutritional deficiency and the danger of physical disintegration remained serious.[19]

---

[17] P. 46
[18] Op.cit.
[19] P. 143

This view was further strengthened by Amin (1990), who observed that whereas the 1960s were characterised by the great hope of seeing an irreversible process of development launched through what came to be called the Third World and Africa particularly, the subsequent period presented disillusionment. According to the author, development in Africa had broken down; its theory was in crisis; and its ideology was the subject of doubt.[20] Particularly, the author noted that Africa's backwardness had its origins in the lack of an agricultural revolution, which was an essential precondition to development. However, while the author had assessed the situations, he failed to appreciate Africa's problems as deriving from the fundamental lack of human rights on the continent. It is the lack of enjoyment of these that led to the decline that we see on the continent.

While challenging the view that Western economic growth and prosperity ahead of other areas arose from availability of local natural resources, Rosenberg and Birdzell (1987) observe that explanations like these are likely to meet the difficulty that a society's economic resources are not its natural resources, *"but a relation, internal to the society, between its natural resources and its organizational and technological skills in extracting or otherwise acquiring and utilizing those natural resources for advancing its people's material welfare."*

The authors point out that resources that contribute to economic wealth are usually not simply material, but *"a subtle combination of materials present in nature, with the human knowledge and social organization required to use those materials . . . to satisfy human needs."* Quoting the American Plains Indians,

---

[20]   P. 1

for example, the authors observe that the oil, coal, iron ore, forests, and farmlands of North America were not economic resources to them, but the buffalo herds were resources of utmost importance. The authors note that the West's economic resources are merely its wealth (capital); however, the problem is how the West generated the organizational and technological skills required to produce and exploit that wealth."[21]

Based on the above argument, therefore, one can see that emphasis on economic development in Africa, while ignoring fundamental human rights, is often misplaced. In other words, stress should rather be put more on human freedom.

Hyden (1983) has observed that as Africa's new states were (in the 1980s) reaching the age of a human generation, few could look back on a period of real progress. According to the author, there were countries that had experienced real *per capita* economic growth, and where a large number of people rightly felt they were better off than at independence. However, many other countries on the continent had recorded negative growth and declining real *per capita* income.[22]

The author noted that while Ghana and Uganda, for instance, were considered countries of great promise in the early 1960s—with well-developed small-holder agriculture and enjoying the benefit of a large pool of relatively highly educated and experienced citizens, following a range of ill-conceived policies and falls in world market prices—the two were caught in a vicious circle of stagnation. This seriously limited the scope for any improvement in the foreseeable

---

[21]   Ibid, p.10
[22]   P. xi

future. According to the author, a range of other African countries of varying ideological outlooks also shared the fate of Ghana and Uganda in varying degrees.

However, the author failed to notice one thing that Ghana and Uganda, just like the rest of Africa especially south of the Sahara, were largely monocrop economies which heavily depended on foreign markets. In other words, their strength and sustainability were heavily precarious.

The above view was echoed by a conference, *The State and Crisis in Africa*, held at Mweya Safari Lodge in Uganda, May 12-17, 1990. The conference observed that, although at independence, the State in Africa was viewed by nationals and foreigners as having a major role in promoting economic and social development; and while during the first decade and a half after independence, a great deal was achieved on the social, economic, and political fronts; from the mid-1970s onwards, the record of the continent became one of almost constant decline.

According to the conference, average living standards in many countries in sub-Sahara Africa fell below what they were at independence; most of the improvements in the physical quality of life achieved during the 1960s and 1970s were eroded; and by the 1980s, the record was almost everywhere one of abysmal failure. The conference noted that the causes of the crisis were both internal and external:

"Among the internal factors are: the absence of political stability, due primarily to the intervention of the military or to bad leadership; lack of probity, equity, accountability and patriotism; illiteracy; a failure to work out priorities; the straightjacket of the mono-crop economy and a dearth of managerial and financial skills needed for carrying out development programmes; and lack of appropriate technology. External factors have been manifest in the ex-colonial powers' tendency to continue to dominate their former colonies by manipulating internal differences and using economic levers—in particular, depression of prices and the quota system of purchase of primary produce, in order to demand concessions and, at worst to foment discontent and coups d'état."[23]

While the conference had attempted to assess the African crisis, they, nevertheless, failed, in that, instead, they explained the problem away. Their analysis was fundamentally flawed. Why? For, if the reasons for failure of growth and development on Africa were as they analysed, we should have started to see an improvement since this assessment. However, the situation keeps worsening, leading to deepening poverty, human displacement and general degeneration. What this means, therefore, is that there is a bigger explanation than what is imagined.

2.2 Theories of Development in Africa

Writing in the *International Herald Tribune* (Pretoria, South Africa), August 4, 1994, Professor Ali Mazrui proposed re-colonisation of Africa as the solution to the continent's many development problems. The professor noted that much of contemporary Africa was in *"the throes of decay and decomposition,"* such that even the degree of dependent modernisation achieved under colonial rule was being

---

[23] Dag Hammarskjöld Foundation, *The State and the Crisis in Africa: In Search of a Second Liberation*, Uppsala, Sweden, 1992: pp. 7-8

reversed. According to the Professor, the successive collapses of the state in one African country after another had suggested a once-unthinkable solution—re-colonisation:

> "To an increasing number of Africans, this is the bitter message that has emerged from the horrifying events in Rwanda [1994].[24] While Africans have been quite successful in uniting to achieve national freedom, we have utterly failed to unite for economic development and political stability. War, famine, and ruin are the postcolonial legacy for too many Africans. As a result, external re-colonisation under the banner of humanitarianism is entirely conceivable."[25]

Well, while Mazrui may have been irked by the depressing situations on the continent, indeed, the suggestion of re-colonisation was an absurd one. For instance, how would such a process be implemented? By who? Who would be the umpire in order to make sure that the process does not turn expropriational? And when we had been recolonised, wouldn't we return to the cycle of the 1960s, looking for independence again? In other words, this is what is called moving in circles! But Mazrui must be appreciated in that the situations on the continent are so depressing that sometimes one thinks of the very eccentric solution to them.

---

[24] Rwanda faced an ugly genocide in 1994, perpetrated by Hutu ethnic group against especially Tutsi, in a bid to exterminate the latter. It is estimated that close to eight hundred thousand people lost their lives in the holocaust!

[25] A reproduction in *CODESRIA Bulletin*, Number 2, 1995, p. 22

In 1993, the World Bank expressed a similar view as Mazrui's when it noted that while Africa, particularly Sub-Sahara Africa, entered independence with high expectations for rapid economic progress; and whereas in the early years, many African countries successfully expanded their infrastructure and social services, and much effort was spent on consolidating the fragile nation state; following an initial period of growth, most African economies faltered and went into decline.

According to the Bank, overall, Africans became poor in the 1990s as they were thirty years earlier—a situation that had spurred many governments to undertake far-reaching reforms. Nevertheless, even with these reforms, the Bank noted, the experience of the first generation of Africans after independence raised questions such as:

> "Does Africa face special structural problems that have not been properly understood? Has the institutional dimension been neglected? Have the recent reform programs been too narrow or too shallow? Could the process of formulating and implementing reforms be improved? Has the effect of external factors been correctly assessed? Are external assistance and debt relief appropriate and adequate? More fundamentally, is there a long-term vision that is both credible and energizing?"[26]

While the Bank may have made an extensive soul-searching to appreciate the problem, nevertheless, it failed, in that the reference to structural reforms in form of institutional

---

[26] The World Bank, *Sub-Saharan Africa: From Crisis to Sustainable Growth—A Long-Term Perspective Study*, Washington, D.C., 199, P. 1

changes was far beside the point. Moreover, the allusion to external factors, including aid and debt relief, was even more distressing. The problem of Africa is ideological and technological, i.e. the lack of human freedom.

And finally, on his first visit to Africa since election as the first African-American president of the United States, Barack Obama, in his address to the Ghanaian Parliament on July 11, 2009, lamented that Africa had a long way to go. He observed that:

> ". . . I say this knowing full well the tragic past that has sometimes haunted this part of the world. I have the blood of Africa within me, and my family's own story encompasses both the tragedies and triumphs of the larger African story . . . But despite the progress that has been made . . . we also know that much of that promise has yet to be fulfilled. Countries like Kenya, which had a per capita economy larger than South Korea's when I was born [1961], have been badly outpaced. Disease and conflict have ravaged parts of the African continent. In many places, the hope of my father's generation gave way to cynicism, even despair."

The president cautioned that while it was easy to point accusing fingers to other people for the problems of the continent, the real problem was more internal than external:

> "Yes, a colonial map that made little sense, bred conflict; and the West has often approached Africa as a patron rather than a partner. But the West is not responsible for the destruction of the Zimbabwean economy over the last decade, or wars in which

children are enlisted as combatants. In my father's life, it was partly tribalism and patronage in an independent Kenya that for a long stretch derailed his career, and we know that this kind of corruption is a daily fact of life for far too many."

The president reminded his audience that development depended more upon good governance, and this is the ingredient that was lacking in Africa for far too long.[27]

---

27 "Obama Ghana Speech: Full Text" at http://www.huffingtonpost. com/2009/07/11/obama-ghana-speech-full-t_n_230009.html. Barack Obama became the first elected African-American (black) President of the United States on Tuesday, November 5, 2008.

3

THE IMPLICATIONS OF THE ABOVE SITUATIONS ON THE CONTINENT

3.1 Socio-Economic and Political Decline

While a number of authors and researchers have looked at decline in Africa as a phenomenon of today, decline in Africa commenced with the onset of colonialism in the nineteenth century. Brett[28] has observed that control over advanced mechanical and social technology enabled the West to extend an empire over most of the world by the end of the nineteenth century where its demands broke open old societies. According to the author, soldiers and administrators had to be paid; commerce to make profits; railways to carry produce; and missionaries provided with converts to *literate* religions:

> "As capital, administration and Church followed the explorers and soldiers, functioning colonies emerged controlled by light-skinned people with an absolute faith in the superiority of their culture and of their corresponding right to rule the dark-skinned inhabitants. This process initiated a continuing

---

[28] Op. cit

revolution of many phases, many styles and many implications. External dominance and internal dependence created a situation which inevitably transformed the entire social fabric of the people whose countries are now underdeveloped."[29]

According to the author, export-oriented economies had to be created, traditional social structures modified, and existing political authorities made to accept their subordination to the foreign invader. This, according to the author, occurred under systems of indirect rule as under direct rule. The author goes on that:

"In the latter, no real attempt was made to reduce the impact of the new forces upon existing structures; in the former they generally conflicted with, and undermined traditional practice. To the extent that chiefs were able to assimilate the bureaucratic norms established by the central government, they became alienated from their subjects. Equally significant, these changes in social, economic and political structures meant the emergence of new social forces in indigenous society whose interests could be expected to conflict on many levels with those of both the colonial and traditional elites. Although it may have dragged individuals and peoples through blood and dirt, through misery and degradation in the process, imperialism in Africa as in Asia began to fulfil a double mission ... one destructive, the other regenerating—the annihilation of old Asiatic society,

---

[29] P. 1

and the laying of the material foundations of Western society in Asia."[30]

According to the author, while Europe created the enlightenment at home, its subjects extracted the wealth of the tropics by murder, torture, and deceit:

"As a result, Europe is often seen as the builder of underdevelopment, not development; the imitation of European models—an invitation to mortifying setbacks, not the key to progress. And these facts cannot be isolated from the work of academic model-builders, because the achievements of Western social thought have been as potent an instrument of control as its military and industrial technology. Western culture, dominated by the scientific approach in this sphere as in many others, has claimed and enforced a general superiority to any and all other systems of civilised life. Whatever, his past achievements, colonised man was made to learn the colonial culture, to study the histories of Europe and not his own, because he was told that there was no African history to teach ... only the history of Europeans in Africa. And there can be little doubt that these assumptions were widely accepted; this cultural dominance created a dependence complex, which led many colonial peoples to accept the characteristics assigned to them by the dominant group. To the extent that they did so, they denied themselves the possibility of liberation; instead of resisting they manned the armies and carried the guns, which maintained the colonial system. If the acceptance of

---

[30] Ibid

Western assumptions and of the associated political and economic linkages with the West was the source of their powerlessness, how can theory based upon the

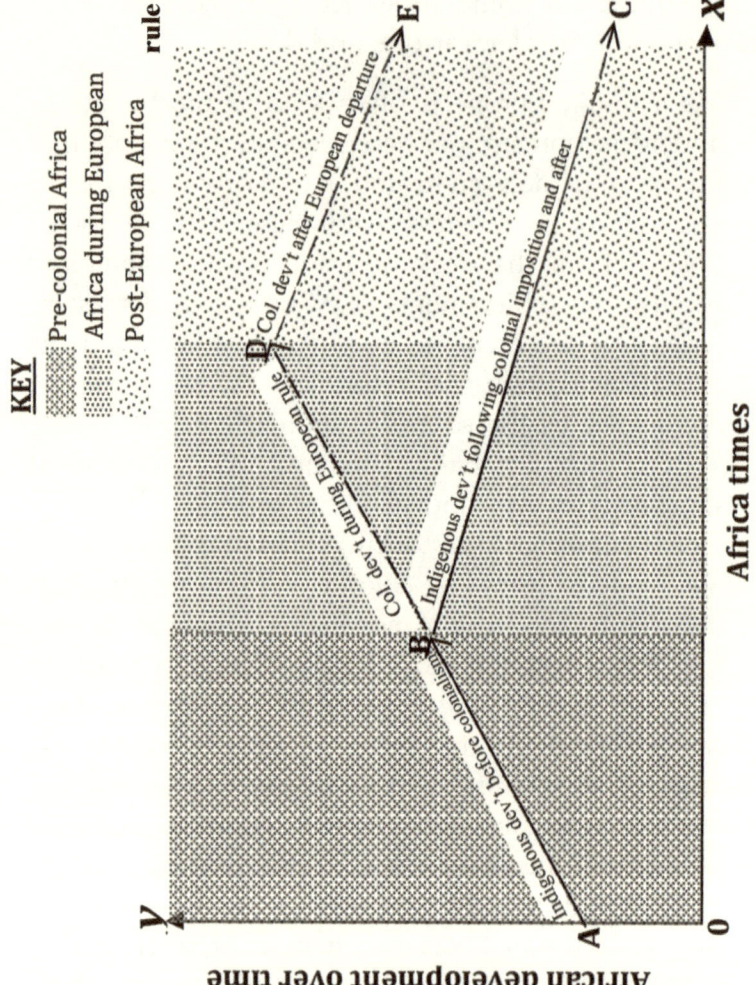

Fig 1: A Graphical Illustration of the Aftermath of Colonial Imposition in Africa

need to imitate Western achievements serve to free them from their underdevelopment?"[31]

This account goes to underline one fact that indeed social, economic, and political decline in Africa started with the imposition of colonialism. In which case, decline in Africa has been more enduring than is usually thought.

The above graph shows that while Africa was developing on its own accord before colonial imposition in the nineteenth century (line segment AB), following imposition, the trend became one of continuous reversal (line segment BC). And while the Europeans were here, they established their own version of development in terms of the new roads, schools, hospitals, administrative structures, factories, etc. (dotted line segment BD). However, this later development was strictly dependent on European presence on the continent because only they understood it and could sustain it. This is why as soon as they left, this so-called development also went into decline (dotted line segment DE).

This dependent development, as Professor Ali Mazrui has termed it, was at its utmost in the early 1960s when a number of African states alleged to have become independent. However, following years of imagined independence and self-rule, this was ran down. Thus, while it may appear that the 1960s were better off for Africa in terms of gross domestic products (GDPs), socio-economic infrastructure, and relative peace and stability, this was false development because it was not founded on internal socio-economic and political growth. In other words, this basically relied on the presence of the Europeans on the continent.

---

[31]   P. 9

But the above graph reveals another fact that it is upon our indigenous development that the colonialists built their own. When Africans saw the nice roads, hospitals, schools, etc., they were deceived to believe that this was their own development. In fact, it was not. In real terms, we had been in freefall decline since the onset of colonialism. This is what otherwise explains the anarchy on the continent in terms of the incessant wars, civil instabilities, hunger and starvation, disease and deepening poverty. And if the trend is not reversed, we are headed for real extinction.

3.2 The Human Rights Situation on the Continent

3.2.1 Human Rights Understanding and Practice on the Continent

While writing on *Democratization and the Protection of Human Rights in Africa*, Ambrose (1995) noted that as Africans reflect on the past and ponder their future, democracy and respect for human rights have come to be seen as the sole means of redemption for a people who since independence have been forced to live with the tyranny of dictators and despots:

> "All over the continent, Africans have experienced the woes of gross abuses inflicted by military dictators and self-styled life presidents. Under the leadership of these regimes, Africans have witnessed massive corruption, human rights abuses, and economic deprivations that have caused more than 265 million people to live in absolute poverty. Africans are overwhelmingly convinced that the root cause of their dilemma is the absence of good governance and accountability by their leaders. Therefore, Africans

expect democracy to replace guns with butter, poverty with plenty; and want to a life of hope and dignity."[32]

But the author adds that while Africans need democracy, liberal democracy is not their best option:

> "…Africans should be allowed to decide on a democracy that suits Africa's reality. Poverty presently grips over 265 million people, and the continent is constantly plagued by ethnic tension. In addition, the continent's external debt stands at more than $270 billion. Unlike what is prescribed for Africa, liberal democracy was successfully attained in western countries because those countries had already attained a level of economic development. In addition, there is confusion as Africans attempt to install a western system within existing traditional structures and cultural practices. Consequently, the current democratization exercise will not result in the social, political, and economic transformation that Africa needs."[33]

While the author was possibly right that the current socio-cultural settings in Africa may not permit liberal or western style democracy, the author was wrong to insinuate that Africans are possibly species that cannot change. Like other humans, Africans can change and develop. However, the problem in Africa is not poverty or the cultural settings, but an imposed state. In an environment where groups (ethnic) identify separately and each is always struggling to be free from the others, no one

---

[32] P. xv

[33] Preface, p. xii

can achieve popular consensus or acceptance. The most that is expected in this situation is anarchy, which translates into unending wars and conflict that characterise the continent. Therefore, to insinuate that Africans cannot possibly adopt liberal or western style democracy is fundamentally flawed.

Furthermore, the author argues that since liberal democracy is not Africa's best option, the people should be left to decide a democracy that suits their reality. Indeed, this, too, is absurd because democracy must have a stable meaning, not a wanton one. But that aside, the author risks playing in the hands of vicious dictators like Yoweri Museveni of Uganda; the late Julius Nyerere of Tanzania; Robert Mugabe of Zimbabwe; Kamuzu Banda of Malawi; Mobutu Seseko of Zaire; and a host of others who have maintained that Africa should be left for Africans. These politicians come-academicians have argued that Africa should be left to chart its own course of democracy and development. For instance, in his *What is Africa's Problem?*, Yoweri Museveni of Uganda, since 1986 to date, has argued that while one of the problems plaguing the state in Africa has been lack of democracy and accountability, the talk about democracy should not be confused with multi-party politics. He argues:

> "When I talk about democracy, I should not be confused with those who are talking about multi-parties. The talk about multi-parties is about form, not about substance. Each country's circumstances should dictate what form of democratic expression should be used ... I do not agree with those who are trying to push the idea of multi-parties down everybody's throats."[34]

---

[34] Yoweri Museveni, while addressing the Dag Hammarskjöld Foundation Conference held at Mweya Safari Lodge in Uganda,

But this was in 1990 when Yoweri Museveni had already spent four years in power, following a guerrilla war that brought him in, in 1986. Yet Museveni has continued to rule Uganda to-date; and in 1996, he is believed to have rigged elections to extend himself in power for another five years in addition to the ten he had already ruled since 1986. In fact, in 1996 he used the military and the law to rig himself to power, by, on one hand, threatening war if he lost the election, and on the other, banning free competition based on political pluralism. In addition, in the 2001 election and subsequent ones, Yoweri Museveni also rigged elections in Uganda. For instance, in the election petitions twice brought by his three-time main political challenger, Retired Col. Dr. Kizza Besigye, the Supreme Court of Uganda held that the elections were marred by serious irregularities including (in the words of Chief Justice Odoki):

> [In 2001] "... the 2nd Respondent [the Country's Electoral Commission] *did not comply with the provisions of the Presidential Elections Act"*: *"in s. 28, ... it did not publish in the Gazette 14 days prior to nomination of candidates, a complete list of polling stations that were used in the election"*; *"in s. 32 (5), ... it failed to supply to the Petitioner official copy of voters register for use by his agents on polling day"*; *"in some areas of the country, the principle of free and fair election was compromised"*; *"in the special Polling Stations for soldiers, the principle of transparency was not applied"*; and *"there was evidence that in a significant number of Polling Stations there was cheating."*[35]

May 13, 1990. The address was reproduced in a compilation of his speeches and writings, entitled, *What is Africa's Problem?* (p. 193).

[35] Rtd. Col. Dr. Kizza Besigye vs. Electoral Commission & Yoweri Museveni - Supreme Court of Uganda Presidential Election Petition

In 2006, the same Chief Justice noted:

> "... *disenfranchisement of voters by deleting their names from the voters register or denying them the right to vote*"; "*bribery and intimidation or violence in some areas of the country*"; "*the principles of equal suffrage, transparency of the vote, and secrecy of the ballot were undermined by multiple voting and vote stuffing in some areas ...*"[36]

Following the 2011 presidential elections—a fourth under Yoweri Museveni—seven out of the eight former presidential candidates unanimously agreed that he, in connivance with the country's Electoral Commission, had massively rigged the elections, which one of the candidates, Nobert Mao, sadly described as "... *a manifestly flawed process ... which could only be categorized as a coup against the people of Uganda*"!

Therefore, if we should—in the words of Yoweri Museveni—talk about substance and not the form of democracy, then what substance would this be when a man sets out to rule indefinitely amidst perpetually rigged elections? The argument that every African country should be left to chart its own course of democracy—as often advanced by many an African ruler and academicians—is, therefore, not only dishonest, but also fraudulent. More so, it is a gross violation of human rights.

Lomo (2000) has observed that despite its vast wealth of natural resources, Africa remains a continent beset by multiple crises:

No. 01 of 2001 [Kampala Law Reports (KALR) 2001].

[36] Rtd. Col. Dr. Kizza Besigye vs. Electoral Commission and Yoweri Museveni—Supreme Court of Uganda Presidential Election Petition No. 01 of 2006.

"Since the colonial rulers transferred political power to African successors, many countries (especially south of the Sahara) have experienced dramatic changes, including forceful recasting of institutions and violent change of leadership. Despite its abundant wealth of natural resources, Sub-Sahara Africa is economically very poor. In 1999, the estimated combined gross domestic product (GDP) of all Sub-Saharan countries excluding South Africa was a mere $300 billion, less than that of the Netherlands. In 1999, the region's foreign debt was estimated at $227 billion. African countries, especially those south of the Sahara, suffer not only from weak economies but also deteriorating terms of trade with the rest of the world."[37]

According to the author, at the beginning of the second millennium, much of Africa was engulfed in interstate and civil wars, plus ethnic conflicts, which had precipitated massive waves of displacement both within and outside the affected countries. However, the author notes that displacement is not only caused by wars and ethnic conflict, but so-called development and conservation projects, and the restructuring of economies have displaced many urban and rural poor from their homes, and forced people to live in abject poverty. The author also notes that recent semblances of democratization in Africa, notwithstanding the conflicts on the continent, are often symptomatic of the dire human rights situation.[38]

Writing on election failure in Africa in *The Sunrise* (Uganda), January 11-18, 2008, Moses Walubiri observed

---

[37]   P. 269
[38]   P. 270

that there are only a paltry number of countries on the continent where elections are often held without a lapse into mayhem orchestrated along tribal or ethnic lines:

> "Due to the intransigencies of those who, despite the murkiness of African politics, rig elections; a big price has always had to be paid in terms of ruined economies and festered deep-seated tribal animosities, leading to genocide and pogroms. It is quite tragic that politicians, for purely selfish interests, play the tribal card in their incessant struggles to outsmart their rivals in the political realm. The simple fact that the countries they lead are bigger than they are or grander than their personal interests tends to elude them … Ironically, those that are usually decimated like vermin are the poor souls whose life is a daily struggle for survival."[39]

According to Gingyera-Pinycwa (1998), internal conflicts based on ethnicity, tribalism, bad governance, and poverty have been the root causes of flight and internal displacement of large numbers of people in Africa. The author observes that with direct colonialism gone *the mother of the root causes now stands out as internal conflict based on ethnicity, tribalism, bad governance, and poverty*:

> "… Each factor gives rise to internal strife which has led to … the flight of large numbers of people outside their national territories; and the flight or displacement of large numbers of people from their usual natural areas of habitation. By and large, Africans are to blame for what is happening in the matter of refugees and

---

[39] "Tribalism and the Tragic Tale of Africa's Stolen Elections," *The Sunrise* (Uganda), January 11-18, 2008, p. 12.

internally displaced people. In particular, one cannot help deprecating and condemning the stubbornness, arrogance and stiff-necked approaches with which internal differences are handled by its politicians. The result has been failure, even where there could be success, to contain differences that result in the internal strife that sends so many innocent and helpless people away from their homes."[40]

However, according to the author, tragically for Africa, such uprooted and displaced people are now no longer as politically inert or helpless as they have always been expected to be:

"They now obtain arms and acquire military skills in order to retaliate against regimes that forced them to flee from their homes. They have become "in the terminology of Aristide Zolberg and his colleagues, 'refugee warrior communities.'" This is what the Rwandese in Uganda [in 1990] and the Rwandese in Zaire [in 1996] became. 'Even when inside their countries of birth ... they may now do the same.' In either case, conflicts that might be limited are extended. They simply drag endlessly on. Regardless of the origin of the internal conflict, it inevitably attracts foreign intervention. The consequences are fairly known—more internally displaced people; more sufferings and abuse of human rights, as the internal strife and the internally induced conflicts impact on the people."[41]

---

[40] P. 48-49
[41] P. 49

However, I must add that the author's assessment of the problem is a little inadequate in that the focus on especially internal (read ethnic) strife, ethnicity, and so-called tribalism is rather a focus on symptoms than actual causes. These are mere offshoots of the colonial legacy in Africa: thus the later being the actual root cause.

According to Abdullahi (1997), few African governments openly acknowledge that they violate human rights, because to do so could be self-destructive and dangerous to the interests of the state. The author notes that:

> "Protection of human rights is espoused in every African state as a national duty in which the interest of the regime forms the axis around which human rights issues spin. And on assuming power, most regimes make political capital out of the excesses of their predecessors in government. Thus, whereas policy-makers and statespersons loudly advocate the protection of human rights, the sad reality is that significant abuse of human rights occurs. In some instances, such abuse takes place on a massive scale."[42]

And while commenting on the rule of law in Africa, Gutto (1997) observed that the illegitimacy and crisis of the state and society in Africa requires a reconstruction of society and the theory of rule of law in order to incorporate social justice and increased formal participation of the organised non-state sections of the citizenry. According to the author:

> "... the crises that Africa has undergone have had their positive aspects. They have supplied an opportunity

---

[42] P. 1

for identifying that the paths to social development pursued since independence are inhibitive to the progress of the rule of law and, more importantly, that within the African society there exist forces of resistance and progress that could be used in reconstructing new paths of social development."[43]

The author argues that the state and society of the future in Africa cannot be expected to promote the rule of law and human rights as long as political organisation is viewed simply as a triangle of the legislature, the executive, and the judiciary. According to the author, society and the state must be transformed and reconstructed to constitute a quintuple of the three traditional branches of government operating under modern humane values, plus two additional sides that are usually omitted from the rule of law and human rights paradigm.

These, according to the author, are social justice and an organised citizenry with legal space for direct participation in the governance of society. However, the author fails to appreciate that in Africa, there is never a separation of powers along any so-called traditional branches of government. Everything on the continent is often fused and rotates around the personality of one person – the ruler; and the arguments that there should be social justice and citizens' participation, therefore, cannot hold.

---

[43]   P. 130

4

HUMAN RIGHTS AND
DEVELOPMENT IN UGANDA: A CASE STUDY

4.1 Country Background

4.1.1 Location

Uganda is a country in East Africa, situated along the equator and falling on coordinates of 1° North Latitude and 32° East Longitude. It covers an approximate area of 91,133 square miles or 236,036 square kilometres. It is bordered to the east, by the state of Kenya; to the south, by the states of Tanzania and Rwanda; to the west, by the Democratic Republic of Congo (DRC); and to the north, by the newly formed state of Southern Sudan. The country lies entirely between the two arms of the Great Rift Valley of East Africa.

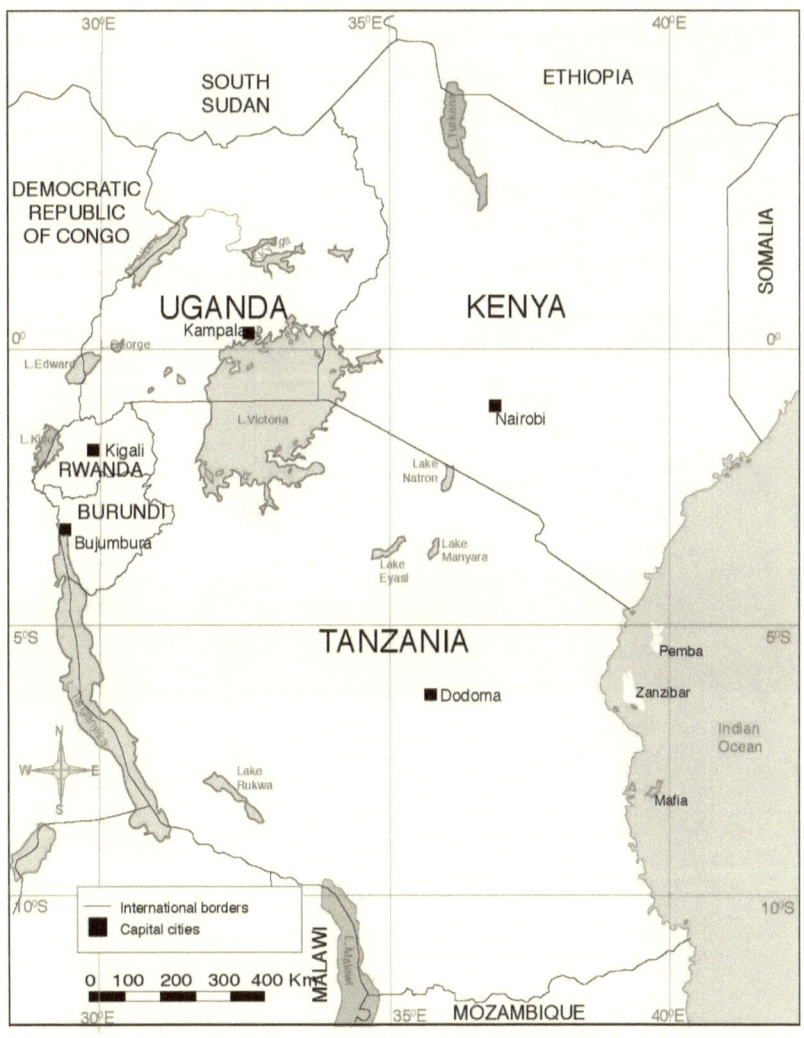

Fig 2: Uganda in East Africa *Fountain Atlas for Uganda Primary Schools*, Fountain Publishers Ltd, Kampala, 2012, p. 46.

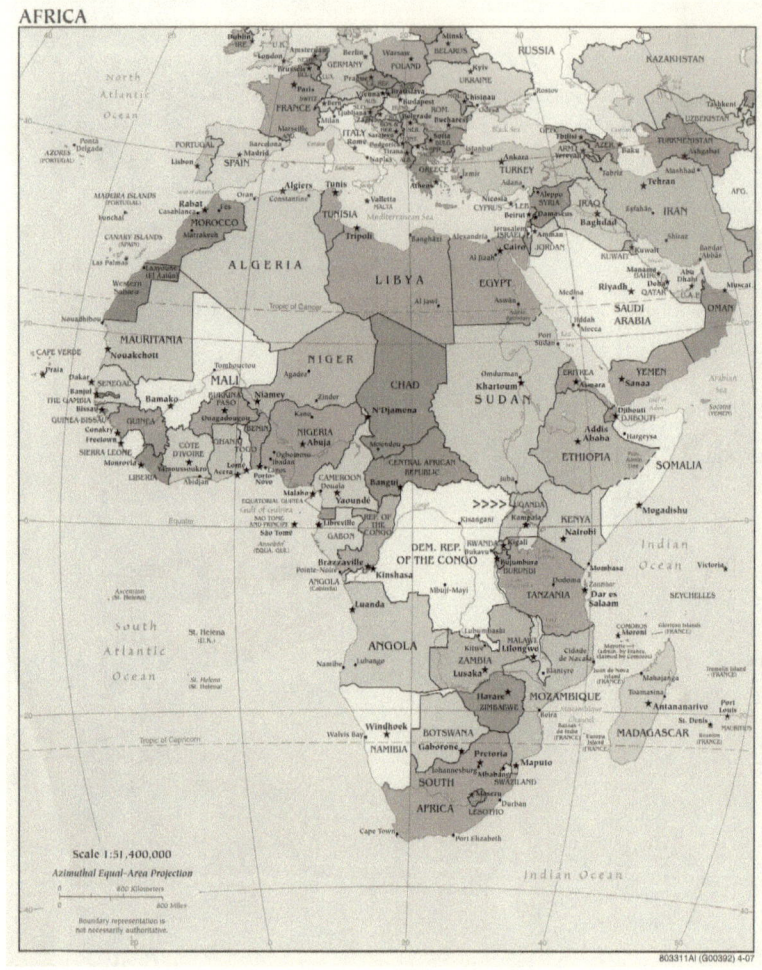

Fig 3: Uganda in Africa The University of Texas Libraries, The University of Texas at Austin.

4.1.2 Social Composition

Uganda has approximately fifty ethnic groups, which can be classified into four broad categories: *Bantu, Nilotics,*

Nilo-Hamites, and *Sudanics*.[44] According to Lamwaka (1998), each of these broad categories speaks a language separate from and generally not understood by the others. According to Wairama (2001), Uganda is comprised of fifty-six formerly independent traditional societies or ethnic groupings, with a few groups who have their origins elsewhere, such as the Nubians *(Sudanic)* and Ugandan Asians. According to Mwambutsya-Ndebesa, there is no Ugandan culture, but there are as many cultures as there are peoples.[45]

Figure 4 below provides an approximate shade of the peoples of Uganda in 1962 when the country became so-called independent.

---

[44] Sudanics are an extension of their fellow *Sudanic* stock in Southern Sudan; and in Uganda they constitute groups like the *Madi, Toposa, Nubians, Kakwa, Alur, Luluba*, etc. (Wairama, 2001; http://en.wikipedia.org/wiki/Southern_Sudan).

[45] A preface to *Peoples and Cultures of Uganda* (cited above).

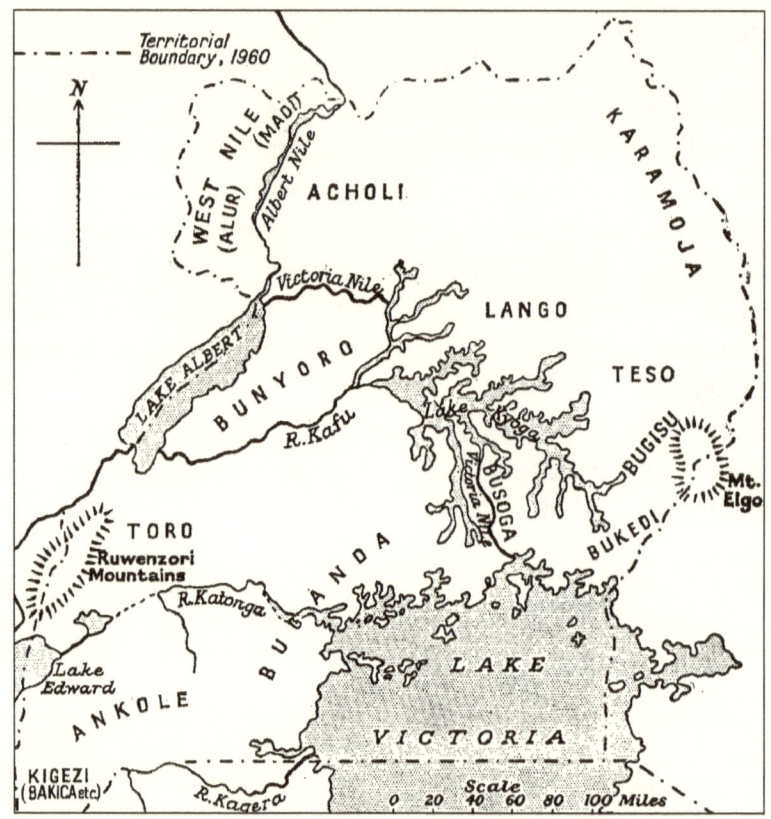

Fig 4: Boundaries and peoples of Uganda in 1962 *A History of East Africa*, Kenneth Ingham, Pearson Education Limited, London (1962), p. 434.

4.1.3 Uganda's Political History

Kabwegyere (1974) observes that Uganda came into being as a geo-political unit during the period of intensified expansion of the European States and, in particular, during the expansion of England:

"This was a period of struggle for colonies, a struggle for economic territories. It was a time of export:

44

export of capital for investment; export of population for settlement; export of culture, cultural imperialism. This was a period during which non-Western peoples were brought under the domination of the West."[46]

According to the author, the pre-colonial era in Uganda was characterised by diversity in terms of social scale and social organisation:

"In terms of social scale, there were the powerful kingdoms of Buganda and Bunyoro Kitara, whose citizens numbered millions at the height of their power. Kingship was the very core source of cohesion and ordering of the governmental structure. These states had armies as instruments of conquest and defence. Bunyoro and Buganda often quarrelled and went to war; the British found the two in open quarrel and used this to their own advantage ... There were other numerous kingdoms, including those that were amalgamated to make Ankole kingdom and the principalities that were brought together to form Busoga territory. Toro kingdom formed a special category in that it was a subsidiary of Bunyoro Kitara. In terms of social scale, these were second to the large-scale Bunyoro and Buganda ... The rest of Uganda's peoples were organised in small scale, non-centralised societies."[47]

According to Nabuguzi (1994), the 1900 Agreement with Buganda marked the start of effective British control of the current Uganda territory:

---

[46] p. 1
[47] Pp. 21-22

"The agreement created a state within a state, by giving preferential treatment to Buganda vis-à-vis other regions in the colony. Its traditional institutions were preserved; Buganda notables were rewarded with large tracts of land in freehold land tenure. The *batongole* and *bakungu* chiefs retained administrative control of their territory, although power was transferred from the king to an oligarchy of Christian chiefs whose appointment was approved by the colonial forces. The authority of these chiefs, who did not belong to the traditional hierarchy, was strengthened by the award of *mailoland* (large tracts of land measured in miles). A lesser degree of autonomy was given to kings in other kingdom areas like Toro, Ankole and Bunyoro."[48]

According to the author, the hierarchical Buganda kingdom was imposed everywhere else, even over segmentary societies to the east and the north:

"... By using religious criteria to appoint chiefs in Buganda, the religious dimension to the distribution of power was institutionalised ... the system engendered regional rivalries and resentments between Buganda, the other kingdom areas in Western Uganda and the Northern and Eastern regions. In a *divide and rule* policy, Baganda, [Batoro] and Banyoro chiefs, as well as Nubian soldiers, were employed as administrators in territories outside their own, creating multiple relationships of mutual ethnic resentment. Bunyoro was dismembered and its counties given to Buganda. Baganda agents like

---

[48] P. 113

Semei Nyanzi and *Kakungulu* were used to subordinate other parts of Uganda. Buganda enjoyed a greater degree of autonomy in its internal rulership than other parts of Uganda. Districts and Local Administrations built on ethnic lines made the ethnic and regional entity the centre of political activity."[49]

However, the author notes that in reality, these local administrations never corresponded to the pre-colonial forms of authority or territorial political divisions:

"The colonial state created traditional chiefs where they did not exist to administer territorial units that were often equally artificial. This was consistent with a policy of creating political units whose legitimacy was closely tied to the colonial order. Even where traditional chiefs predated colonial rule, the British distorted their original functions and domain, demoting former kings to *saza chiefs* (Bulamogi in Busoga), elevating segmentary clan heads to hierarchical county chiefs (Lango, Teso, and Bugisu), enlarging kingdoms (Buganda, which was the beneficiary of territory of the severed Bunyoro kingdom), and amalgamating chiefdoms (West Nile, Busoga, Acholi). Fluid groupings were transformed into ethnic constructions with well defined territory and leadership."[50]

According to the author, the colonial government adopted the Anglican religion as the undeclared religion of the state:

---

[49] Pp. 113-114
[50] P. 114

"In Buganda, Anglican chiefs were dominant. The
Kabaka (kings) were crowned in the chapel of the
Anglican missionary school of Budo, built near the
traditional Buganda coronation site. Anglican and
Catholic missionary schools were subsidized by the
state but Koranic schools were not. Graduates of these
schools were not accepted in the civil service. Muslims
cut off by the colonial education sought employment
as tax drivers, butchers, and traders. There was a strong
feeling that they were the vanquished of the colonial
era, a feeling that was not helped by the discrimination
to which they were subjected in society."[51]

The author goes further to note that ethnic vertical
differentiation and the fragmentation of political units
heightened ethnic tensions, and these bases of conflict
were to be politicised in the post-colonial period and used
as a rallying platform for interfactional competition for the
control of state resources:

"These were to prove to be the major obstacle in the
nationalist era and in the post-colonial struggles for
various freedoms and rights."[52]

According to a report by *The African Commission's Work
Group on Indigenous Populations*,[53] Uganda was a colony for
over fifty years, during which the British exerted its supreme

---

[51] Pp. 114-115

[52] P. 115

[53] African Commission on Human and Peoples' Rights (ACHPR),
Report of the African Commission's Work Group on Indigenous
Populations/ Communities: Research and Information Visit to the
Republic of Uganda, 14-17, 24-29, July 2006.

economic and civilising mission, and effectively abrogated the traditional systems of social and political organisation by subordinating them to the foreign system.

"The strategic location of Uganda at the headwaters of the Nile generated a great deal of interest in the West generally, and in the United Kingdom more specifically, insofar as its control would assure the security of Egypt, which was the priceless crown in the colonial economic and military master plan for the continent. So great was this interest that the British government invested heavily in the opening up of the Uganda railway, whose construction consumed colossal sums of money and, in its wake, demanded recompense through a more rigorous colonial enterprise and taxation, not only in Uganda itself but in neighbouring Kenya, where exclusive territories were set apart as White highland commercial agricultural development."[54]

According to the source, colonial domination in Uganda took the form of indirect rule, *which, in its most pristine form, ensured minimum disruption of local socio-political relations to the extent that they were subordinated and responsive to colonial control and manipulation:*

"As many Ugandan communities were organised along clear social constructs such as chieftaincies or kingships, the role of central government in augmenting social change was undertaken with ease. However, this was not so for some communities, such

---

[54] P. 28

as the Karamojong, whose social agents were out of sync with the colonial mindset, a fact which resulted in a much more aggressive role of the state in reforming the social order of that community. The differences in power exerted by the colonial state over different communities in Uganda constituted an important historical construction of the crisis faced by some of those communities today, such as the Karamojong."[55]

What we learn from the foregoing account is that, as a state, Uganda was invented by the British colonialists beginning the nineteenth century. In other words, it was a creation from without. The purpose of this creation was to control the peoples and the lands of the area in order to exploit them for the metropolitan economy. This is why, when the state had been created, it had to continually be sustained by use of force in order to exist; a situation that persists to-date.

4.1.4 The Socio-Political Environment in Uganda

In order to better assess the condition of the state, it has been important to review the socio-political environment in the country. This has been well presented by Wairama,[56] who has argued that the process of nation-building in Uganda has been complicated by the fact that the current ethnic groups in the country used to be independent traditional societies whose peoples, languages, and territories were originally separate. According to the author, because the ethnic groups in Uganda used to be independent traditional societies whose peoples, languages, and territories were clearly demarcated,

---

[55] P. 5-6

[56] Op. cit

the process of nation-creation without the people's consent has caused obvious problems:

"Today, Bantu-language speakers comprise slightly over two-thirds of the population. They include the Eastern Lacustrine and Western Lacustrine Bantu, living in the populous region of East Africa's Great Lakes. Eastern Lacustrine Bantu-speakers include the Baganda, Basoga, and many smaller societies in Uganda, Kenya, and Tanzania. Western Lacustrine Bantu-speakers include the Banyankole, Banyoro (people of Bunyoro), Batoro, and several smaller groups. The second largest group is the Nilotic people, comprising of Iteso and Karamojong cluster of ethnic groups who speak Eastern Nilotic languages, and the Acholi, Alur, and Langi, who speak Western Nilotic languages. A smaller group of people speaking Sudanic languages, who also arrived in Uganda from the north over a period of centuries, includes the Kakwa, Lugbara, Ma'di, Nubians, and other small groups in the northwest of the country. Uganda also has a large refugee population, including refugees from Burundi, Rwanda, Somalia, and Sudan."[57]

According to the author, the history of Uganda defies many theories on the nature of the pre-colonial and post-colonial state:

"For example, it could be argued that bringing many ethnic groups together need not lead to conflict and can contribute towards making larger and more viable

---

[57] P. 6

51

states, with all groups having minority status. Therefore, multi-ethnic societies should not be any more prone to civil wars and instability than more homogenous states. In Uganda, however, civil wars and political instability have depended on the degree of suffocation of particular groups at particular times: for example, the Acholi (since 1986), the Baganda (1966-86), and Bakonzo and Karamojong cluster since the early twentieth century. When Uganda became independent, Sir Edward Mutesa, the King of Buganda, was elected the first president, and Milton Obote the first prime minister. The decade immediately after Uganda's independence was a time of enormous social and political change, generating social and political tensions. Prime Minister Obote seized control of the government from President Mutesa in 1966 (Obote I government) with the loss of hundreds of Baganda lives. Despite the friction between Buganda and [the] central government, there was no serious negative public opinion against or intolerance of minorities. However, Buganda continued to have strong political differences with Obote's regime; this culminated in the abolition of the Buganda and other traditional monarchies. The ruling ethnic groups of the newly independent state appeared to have adopted a 'winner takes all' approach. On 25 January 1971, Col. Idi Amin, of Kakwa-Lugbara parentage, deposed President Obote, a Langi, in a military coup, and Obote went in exile in Tanzania. Amin's regime fanned negative ethnic and xenophobic sentiments in 1972 when he expelled over 60,000 Asians by giving them 90 days' notice."[58]

---

[58] Ibid

According to the author, Amin also launched a reign characterised by gross human rights abuses, and the torturing and killing of thousands:

"... in 1977 Amnesty International estimated 300,000 dead. The Acholi and Langi, among others, were particularly targeted. After the fall of Amin's regime to a Tanzania army-led force in 1979, a series of interim administrations was ended when Obote made a comeback, leading his Uganda People's Congress Party (UPC) to victory in 1980 elections that opponents claimed were rigged."[59]

According to the author, while the Amin and Obote II regimes were guilty of the politicisation of ethnicity issues, Museveni's National Resistance Movement (NRM) government (since 1986) tried from the start to promote the implementation of group rights, albeit mainly in terms of gender and for short-term political gain:

"Since 1986, government policies have not stopped conflict and the displacement of people, and this conflict and displacement has mainly been in areas occupied by minorities. The NRM regime has been characterised by peace and prosperity in most of the fertile south, and rebel attacks on civilians and armed conflicts between rebels (Lord's Resistance Army [LRA]) and government forces, causing massive population displacement. The economic and social prosperity in the south contrasts sharply with the abductions,

---

[59]   Ibid

landmines, mutilations, rapes, thefts of property, and threats from the LRA active in the northern districts of Gulu and Kitgum since 1986; and to a lesser extent, attacks on civilians by the now defeated West Nile Bank Front (WNBF) in the northwest between 1995 and 1997. The humanitarian problems in those districts that were historically disadvantaged and which are home to the majority of Uganda's minorities and disadvantaged groups remain ... The country's most dispossessed and vulnerable live in the most unstable regions of the country. Insecurity resulting from insurgencies in the west and north, and from cattle rustling in the northeast (Karamoja), is seriously hampering rural development in these areas."[60]

According to the author, while prone to playing a similar role to that played by the colonial state, the Uganda post-colonial state has, through all the rapid and violent changes of government, generally been more unpredictable:

"Many ethnic groups have found in the 'independent' state a more sympathetic instrument for the advancement of their own interests, mainly under the principle of 'winner takes all.' Thus while successive governments have accepted ethnic diversity, they have also suppressed particular ethnic groups in order to promote the interests of the political leader's ethnic group. This has led to a cycle of conflict and violence."[61]

---

[60] Quoting United Nations Humanitarian Coordination Unit (UNHCU), *Humanitarian Update Uganda*, Vol. 2, Issue 9, 27 November 2000.

[61] P. 7

What the above account reveals to us is that there is failure of nation-building in Uganda. While the state was originally built on multiple ethnic groups and with a later hope of nation-building by the so-called post-independence rulers, this was not possible. Differences continue among the peoples, often also fanned by the rulers of the state, with a purpose to divide and rule. But fundamentally, the peoples of the area were always different and separate, which they still are today.

4.2 Implications of the Above Situations on Human Development in Uganda

4.2.1 Socio-Economic Development

Socio-economic development is the sustainable qualitative change in the social and economic wellbeing of a society. This includes a progressive shift from being largely dependent on the basic wants of life, such as food, shelter, water, and health; to higher types, such as education, knowledge, information, and technology. In other words, if development should occur, these conditions must be founded on a society's internal abilities to sustain them. Short of this, it can never be said that a society has developed.

In Uganda today, development remains elusive, especially because of lack of internal abilities to sustain it. The country suffers from chronic institutional and ethnic instabilities, which have often translated into open violence. For instance, following a second evaluation of the *Rattso Commission* 2003-2007,[62] the NORAD Evaluation

---

[62] The *Rattso Commission* 2003-2007 was an intervention by the Norwegian Agency for Development Cooperation (NORAD) through Norwegian NGOs in Northern Uganda over the period

Department (May 2009)[63] established that a number of achievements had been made in the lives of the target communities in the north, including among others, enhanced food security and livelihoods. However, the agency absurdly noted that withdrawal of the Norwegian Development Cooperation could significantly constrain sustainability of the gains attained, especially due to lack of corresponding local resources and an apparent inability by local authorities to commit resources to donor-supported interventions. The agency noted:

"…[despite] the proximity of district-based implementing partners to the target beneficiaries, and the fact that they, unlike the Norwegian NGOs, [would] stay behind even after the Norwegian development cooperation [was] withdrawn, a likely consequence of their weak capacities would be [the] inability to sustain the benefits . . ."[64]

The above revelation served to underline one major fact that Uganda cannot possibly sustain itself on its own resources.

2003-2007, in response to a massive humanitarian catastrophe engendered by the protracted and vicious war between the government of Uganda and the rebels of the Lord's Resistance Army (LRA), which saw large scale destruction of human lives and property, plus the displacement of close to two million people into internally displaced camps.

[63] NORAD is the Norwegian Agency for International Development Cooperation.

[64] Norwegian Agency for Development Cooperation (Norad), *Evaluation of The Norwegian Development Cooperation Through Norwegian Non-Governmental Organisations in Northern Uganda 2003-2007: Evaluation Report 3/2009*: pp. xiii-xv

There is lack of internal ability to organise, leading to impoverishment, disease, hunger and starvation. The country is chronically afflicted by corruption and dictatorship, giving rise to instability and uncertainty that, in turn, further undermine any hope for organisation. As a result, when it comes to political organisation and mobilisation in the country, we often see wars and conflict.

But the report revealed another absurd fact about Uganda, that the country can only be sustained on foreign resources, especially as aid, which reflects in the country's financial budgets over the years, particularly since the alleged independence in 1962. Indeed, foreign governments and agencies have always contributed resources to the country's budgets, which demonstrates internal incapacity to survive. For instance, in 1998, Uganda was the first heavily indebted and poor country to benefit from an international debt-rescue scheme, the *Initiative for Heavily Indebted Poor Countries (HIPC)*, whose objective is to rescue countries that have accumulated non-payable (read unsustainable) foreign debts. At the time, Uganda owed US$3.6 billion in foreign debt, while the estimated GDP at Purchasing Power Parity (PPP)[65] was a paltry US$14.23 billion!

---

[65]   Purchasing Power Parity is an economic standard used to determine the relative value of currencies, especially estimating the amount of adjustment needed for two countries' exchange rates to be equivalent to or at par with each other's purchasing power. It asks how much money would be needed to purchase the same goods and services in the two countries, and uses that to calculate an implicit foreign exchange rate (http://en.wikipedia.org/wiki/Purchasing_power_parity)

5

CONCLUSION AND RECOMMENDATIONS

This section sums up answers to the six main questions raised in the book, i.e.:

a) Why has Africa persistently failed to develop despite its vast natural resources?
b) Why is Africa chronically afflicted by social and political instabilities, giving rise to massive deaths, large population displacements—both internal and external—and the surging poverty, disease, hunger, and starvation?
c) Why does Africa chronically suffer from political dictatorships?
d) Why is Africa increasingly afflicted by financial and political corruption?
e) What do the above situations signify for Africa?
f) What should be done to address the situations?

Question one: Why has Africa failed to develop despite the vast natural resources?

A number of theories have been advanced to address a question like this, including but not limited to inadequate human and natural resources as engines of development on the continent. However, whereas these play a key role in the development of any society, Rosenberg and Birdzell[66] have argued that explanations like these are likely to meet the difficulty that a society's economic resources are not necessarily its natural resources but a relationship internal to the society, between its natural resources and its organizational and technological skills in extracting or otherwise acquiring and utilizing those natural resources for advancing its people's material wellbeing.

> "Resources that contribute to economic wealth are often not simply material, but a subtle combination of materials present in nature, with the human knowledge and social organization required to use those materials to satisfy human needs."[67]

Going by this argument, therefore, it can be stated that neither lack of human nor natural resources explain the dismal situation on the African continent, but the lack of internal organisation to utilise any available resources could be the explanation.

Almond and Coleman (1971) have introduced other dimensions such as the massive Sahara Desert that has, 'in the past', been a formidable barrier to human intercourse on the continent; the historically impenetrable coastline, virtually devoid of natural harbours and throughout its vast length characterized by strong offshore winds, sand bars, and

---

66 Op. cit
67 This has, especially, been advanced by academicians and African rulers on the continent.

inhospitable deserts or mangrove swamp forests; the continent's tropical character, i.e., squarely straddling the equator, where three-quarters of its huge bulk lie within either the tropical rainforest or the tropical savannah; the great African plateau south of the Sahara—a vast and monotonous landscape of level or slightly undulating surfaces broken only by such highland areas as those of Rwanda, Burundi, or Kenya; and the African soil which over large areas is of relatively poor quality.[68]

The authors have argued that these 'distinctive features' have been crucial, if not decisive, factors which have affected Africa's history, its patterns of political organization, and the interrelationships of its peoples—thus giving rise to the historic division between the Mediterranean Africa and Sub-Saharan Africa; the isolation of Sub-Saharan Africa and, in the past, the vulnerability of Africa's peoples to exploitation and domination by external groups; the comparative smallness in scale, the variegated political systems, and the instability of the boundaries of traditional African societies; and the poverty and low density of the population.[69]

While the authors have looked at the African problem more from the geographical perspective, as here can be seen, they have failed to appreciate the role of the contemporary states on the continent. They continue to assert that the lack of intensive and continuous firsthand contact with extra-African cultures meant the absence of enriching and stimulating effects of cultural infusion, particularly at the material level. In addition, they argue that the sheer density of the tropical forest in West Africa and parts of Central Africa decreed small-scale, closely-knit village societies; and on the

---

[68] P. 247

[69] Ibid

vast stretches of the tropical savannah in the east, central, and southern areas, the poor soil and lack of natural boundaries prevented continuous occupation for either agricultural or pastoral purposes.[70] But these do not explain the continued social and economic failures on the continent today. For, if these were the explanations, then we should have started to see efforts geared at resolving them. For, the world has since changed, bringing in advanced technologies for travel and communication; land exploitation whatever the terrain; and scientific advancement in the areas of human medicine, research and others.

However, there are other theories, such as population depletion by slave trade of the sixteenth to eighteenth centuries;[71] an environment, especially tropical, infested with diseases—especially malaria—which was a cause of under-population and a weak population[72]; and a continent sparsely populated by pockets of politically and economically unviable communities, which were unable to defend themselves in the face of external attacks.[73]

Nevertheless, while these theories have been presented, the problem of Africa, especially today, lies more in its contemporary state than in the otherwise inert explanations. Many of these explanations are surmountable, especially in the face of modern science and technology.

---

[70] P. 250

[71] This has, especially, been advanced by academicians and African rulers on the continent.

[72] Especially adduced by the Europeans of the nineteenth century, e.g. Henry Morton Stanley and David Livingstone.

[73] This theory continues to be an argument by modern day African rulers, e.g. Yoweri Museveni of Uganda.

It goes without saying that if the people of the continent are not free to organise; and if they are under perpetual imposition and repression; then they can only eternally struggle to be free. This explains the incessant wars and instabilities on the continent, which, therefore, have resulted in massive deaths, large population displacements—both internal and external—and the rising poverty, disease, hunger, and starvation. These situations will not abate until the state is done away with.

Question three: Why does Africa chronically suffer from political dictatorships?

As night follows day, so is the situation in Africa. Political dictatorship explains the lack of human freedom on the continent. In other words, Africa is like one big prison with cells as the current states on the continent. It is in this structure that the people of the continent are heavily locked up; and it is, therefore, unthinkable that they can attain any freedom.

Question four: Why is Africa increasingly afflicted by financial and political corruption?

The explanation for this is the lack of checks and balances in the circumstances. If the people cannot effectively check their leaders, then insanity must prevail. This explains the otherwise obscene amassment of wealth and power by the likes of President Theodore Obiang of Equatorial Guinea; late Sani Abaca of Nigeria; late Mobutu Sese Seko of former Congo-Kinshasa—now Democratic Republic of Congo (DRC); late Kamzu Banda of Malawi; Arap Moi, formerly of Kenya; Robert Mugabe of Zimbabwe; late Omar Bongo and his son—Ali Bongo—both of Gabon; Denis Sassou N'Guesso of Congo-

Brazzaville; and others in a lengthy line of African dictators. In other words, when the cat is away, mice must play. The owners of the land are technically away, thus the leaders are at large!

Question five: What do the above situations signify for Africa?

If not resolved, the African condition could lead to human extinction on the continent. This means that the people on the continent will continually suffer massive deaths, eventually leading to their actual disappearance from the surface of the earth. Alternatively, they could suffer gross dehumanisation as a result of the fundamental denials of their human rights. In the former case, whole communities disappear from the surface of the earth; while in the latter, they become mere biological substances. In the latter case, they lose intellectual capacity to think, invent, create, or produce for themselves. Instead, they become automata, i.e., living robots in the production processes of other peoples. Examples of related situations abound on Africa today, including the people's now chronic dependence on the so-called cash crops for survival, plus the perpetual dependence on aid.

As Africans, we have always been told that the cash crops are our privileged share of the international market based on our comparative advantage in them. Yet, this is not the best potential we have on the continent. We have opportunities ranging from use of our vast mineral resources, to the fresh waters, to the diverse flora and fauna (especially for science and tourism), to an extensively arable land (especially south of the Sahara)[74]; and in

---

[74] But even the Sahara can be exploited for this, as we have seen in Libya under Gadhaffi.

modern times, to our limitless endowment of sunshine.[75] But this aside, even if we continue to grow the crops, they never actually lift us from our miseries. In Uganda, for instance, the *Daily Monitor* newspaper, of Tuesday, February 26, 2013, carried a report that one kilogram of Uganda's unprocessed (primary product) cotton was selling a miserable US$1 on the international market, which translated into a paltry US$1,000 to a whole tone (1000 kilograms) of the crop! This was not to consider the physical energies, hope and expectation, plus the waiting and possibly better opportunities forgone in terms of more paying crops or other activities on the same land. In other words, even if we continue to grow the crops, our situation does not improve. Instead, it always gets worse with deepening poverty and increased indebtedness.

But there is another angle to the situation of the continent. As Africans, we are often told that the aid we get in terms of development assistance from the developed world is usually a humanitarian gesture to help the poor stand up. Yet even if we continue getting the said aid, we never actually pull out of our miseries. The question then is: If this is not extinction, what is it?

Question six: What should be done to address the situations?

Firstly, the African condition is one of critical international concern. The rampant, unending wars on the continent, for instance, continue to pose a threat to international peace and stability. Increasingly, the international

---

[75] Especially for solar energy.

community has to intervene in the African situation in order to cause peace. But this does not happen because, in the first instance, the situation is more complicated than is usually imagined. The situation of Africa has to do with the imposed state structures on the continent. Because these structures hail from without, they have remained an obstacle to human development. As a result, humanity is in the process of extinction. In recent times, we are beginning to see collapse of whole states, as in the case of the Sudan, Somalia, DRC, Zimbabwe, Liberia, Rwanda, Ivory Coast, etc. And although some of these may stagger on and stand, their basis has already gone. They can no longer command authority as they used to, especially at the time of the so-called independence. Moreover, they have increasingly become a fetter to human peace and stability. In the words of Professor Mazrui and others, they are failed states.

Secondly, the African condition presents a fertile ground for the growth of international terrorism. As the despair on the continent deepens, opportunities for international terrorism heighten. This is because, in the desperate Africans, the perpetrators of international terrorism find easy minds and hands to exploit for their sinister intentions. Moreover, this is not to countenance internal (read domestic) terrorism, which thrives on internal instabilities, unending dictatorships, and the deepening poverty of the people. Both these phenomena explain the situations in the Horn of Africa, West Africa and, increasingly, in other areas of the continent.

What then should be done?

The international community should compel African rulers to relent power to the people. The international community must appreciate that the situation of Africa is a situation of the whole world. For instance, the growing surge of migrants from the continent to the rest of the world today reflects a deeply decaying situation on the continent, but, in addition, it poses a threat not only to human peace and stability in the host countries, but also to human resources there. Poverty and unemployment in those countries must continue to rise, gradually resulting in unbearable circumstances. In which case, therefore, solving the African problem is solving a world problem.

But how can the international community intervene to solve the African condition, well aware of the suspicions underlying the relations between the two worlds?[76]

It is a known fact that not only African rulers but also Africans in general, tend to hold the international community, especially the West, with suspicion. This is because of the white-washing of Africans, by, especially African rulers and misguided academicians on the continent, claiming that the West has always had no good intentions for Africa. Secondly, it is due to the recent colonial history on the continent, that we suspect especially the West. However, the West is not to blame for the ongoing decay on the continent today in terms of intellectual, social, economic, and political decline.

In recent times, we are even beginning to see whole communities go up in flames, as in the case of Rwanda in 1994; Uganda, especially since 1980s to early 2000s; Kenya, following the elections of 2007; the Democratic Republic of Congo, since the fall of Mobutu Sese Seko in 1997 to-

---

[76] Especially, Africans do suspect especially the West as always pursuing imperial interests in Africa.

date; Southern Sudan, since John Garanga rebellion in 1983; Somalia, since the fall of Mohamed Siad Barre in 1991; and West Africa, in terms of periodical breakdowns in countries like Ivory Coast, Sierra Leon, Nigeria, Guinea Bissau, Equatorial Guinea, etc. In other words, if we were to continue claiming that the West is responsible for our miseries, we would be fundamentally flawed and, indeed, we would never pull out of the problems.

What should be the role of the African peoples in self-liberation?

Africans can play a big role by providing views on how they would wish their problems to be solved. This book is one such contribution. But on the whole, there should be massive referenda, especially among the different ethnic groups, in order to allow the people to participate fully and effectively in raising views on how their problems should be solved.

ANNEX ONE:
WHY WE MUST PERISH—A PERSPECTIVE

On March 15, 2013, a colleague approached me on the subject matter of corruption in Uganda. He sought to know whether corruption in the country could ever be stopped, and what must be done to achieve this. His concern followed widespread reports of gross impropriety in the country, involving huge sums of public resources. "What do you think should be done to stop corruption in Uganda?" he inquired. More so, he was intrigued by the fact that there seemed to be more corruption in the time of President Yoweri Museveni than there possibly was in the past regimes. President Yoweri Museveni had come to power in 1986, following a five-year guerilla war against Apollo Milton Obote and later, General Bazillio Lutwa Okello, both of whom had ruled the country from 1981 to January 1986.

I told my colleague that, first of all, what was happening in the time of Yoweri Museveni did not mean that there was no corruption during the past regimes. I stressed that there was a lot of it, especially because the state in Africa, as in Uganda, basically depends on corruption as its pillar for survival. I explained that corruption was the lifeblood that runs through our political systems, especially since the establishment of the colonial state in the nineteenth century.

I added that the subject was as ironical as it was distressing, especially given what the man—now president—came promising to do to achieve good governance in the country. I observed that, indeed, it was disappointing to imagine that there was more corruption in the time of Yoweri Museveni than there possibly was during the past regimes. I observed that this was because, at the beginning, the man had held himself as a modest and transparent ruler who would leave no stone unturned to uplift good governance in Uganda.

Moreover, he had had the fight against corruption as one of the pillars in his blueprint the *Ten Point Programme of NRM* that would guide his leadership. He held himself as humble, often scoffing at the extravagance of the former rulers who basically lived a consumptive lifestyle, always engulfed in merrymaking. In fact, his initial attires as president (some of them Marxist-style), were made in Katwe, a Kampala City suburb that is home to many recycled artisans in the country. He had scoffed at foreign goods that he thought could be made locally in Uganda, and so went ahead to set an example by buying locally-made suits and seats.

I answered my colleague in a vehement negative that corruption could never be stopped in Uganda because it is the fabric on which the state survives. I explained that the problem was so deeply rooted in society that it had come to pass as a culture. I reminded him that there was so much glorification of corruption in the country that those who left public service with only their humble pensions or a few savings on their bank accounts were often regarded as fools. I added (especially having been rubbed by his suggestion that the solution might be to target the youth for education against the ill) that, in fact, the youth had already been badly infected with the disease that they were almost incurable.

I gave him an example of a story by one J. B. Kakooza in the *Daily Monitor* newspaper of Friday, December 16, 2011, where it was reported that a young man at some university in the country had disclosed that he had decided to offer Procurement as a course at university because it would put him in stores where it would be easy to make some money. According to Kakooza, the young man's course choice had been influenced not by the need to learn how to manage stores, but because it would put him in a position "to steal"! I then told my colleague that this also reflected in the governance sectors in the country, where public officials were occasionally interdicted for stealing small amounts of money here and there. Some of these people, I pointed out, were as young as the structures they worked in!

But I also mentioned that, worst of all, seeing how big thieves in government were being glorified by society, for being 'hardworking and generous', this could not have left the young behind. The corrupt were the richest in society; they lived affluent lives and offered the fattest donations in churches and at other social functions. Most of all, based on their loot, they always won elections, ostensibly to represent the people further! So, I wondered, why the youth wouldn't follow suit! My colleague's final question was: "What then should be done?"

I reminded him that, first of all, corruption was possibly as old as humanity; and it exists in all systems in the world. However, I added that the difference between other systems and ours was that others had efficient and effective mechanisms to detect and prosecute the problem. Moreover, there was not just the mechanisms to fight the problem but also the will. I told him that despite the fact that we had police to fight the problem, there were weaknesses in our system which were as a result of poor interest in fighting the problem, plus inadequate training and facilitation. I mentioned that this affected other institutions in the country as well.

I pointed out, that, for instance, it would be unthinkable for an officer to leave home on an empty stomach, and walk distances to investigate crime, including corruption. Many times officers did not have enogh to eat home, let alone vehicles or equipment to investigate crimes. I pointed out that there were many times when crime registers at police stations were mere exercise books bought by individuals at the stations. Sometimes, staff didn't have pens to write with, and would be seen running around looking for some to borrow, even from the accused criminals! My colleague then reminded me of the squalid conditions in which police lived; to which I swore I could never be seen leaving from in the morning or returning to in the evening, were I a public official. This, I argued, was because, as a public official, I deserved better.

I told him that our problem may have started with the coming of the Europeans, but it grew with the demise of the European state here. When the Europeans were here (I maintained), there was not as much corruption in the local systems as now, except the major one where our people were collectively regarded as non-worth and relegated to simple exploitables. I reminded him that if money was allocated for a road then, it had to do exactly that.

However, I argued that the problem ran wild when the Europeans left and our beloved liberators in black skins stepped in. Then it was no longer the whites (Europeans) against blacks (Africans), but Batoro (my people) against Baganda (the people of Buganda), against Acholi (the people of Acholi), against Banyakore (the people of Ankore), against Bamasaaba (the people of Masaaba), etc. In these circumstances, I argued, it was no longer possible to be transparent and accountable since insular interests had to set in. I emphasised that this was only natural because, in the final analysis, we were different. I went on to caution my colleague that perhaps we had not yet seen corruption in our circumstances, as a lot more was yet to come.

I explained that corruption abhors institutions and erodes institutions. I pointed out that when the Europeans had left, our concerns ceased being open and across the board. Instead, we became ethnically-oriented, i.e. in-ward looking. I told him that usually if a problem is not healed at the start, it is bound to grow. In this case, corruption grew because it was never stemmed at the start. In other words, we should, in the first place, have not inherited the alien systems, but should have discarded them at the time the Europeans left. Only this way would it have been possible to hold our leaders accountable, because then we would know who would lead us and lead us for what. But as long as we failed to do this at the start, it was no longer possible to fight corruption. In other words, corruption in Africa, as in Uganda (I maintained), is a phenomenon of *Who accounts to who?*

I further pointed out that the colonial state we inherited at the start was such a huge bite for us to swallow that it had to choke us. This is why it was not possible to fight corruption because the interests were varied and diverse. I cautioned my colleague that time was coming when people would stab others on open streets and get away with it. This, I argued, would happen because there would be no system in place to check the situation. I closed by reminding my colleague that even as we spoke, there were several murders in the country that were either not known or investigated. This was because of the inherent inability of the state to fight crime.

ANNEX TWO:
THE SIGNIFICANCE OF THE BOOK TO OTHER PEOPLES IN THE WORLD—THE ARAB WORLD

The present book has established an extinction process taking place in Africa as a result of the fundamental denial of human rights on the continent. The purpose of this annex, therefore, is to determine whether the African situation presents parallels to other areas in the world. The preferred area for focus here is the Arab world.

Why the Arab world?

The choice of the Arab world is influenced by the fact that every time one switches on international media, including news channels that are usually regarded as Arab-leaning, e.g. Al Jazeera TV, what is often observed in the Arab world are smoking guns, suicide bombings, human massacres and extensive destruction of property. Most of these are done in the name of the defence of Islam, but sometimes the acts arise out of ethnic or clanal struggles for power. Consequently, uncountable numbers of people continue to lose their lives in this part of the world, and human flesh and blood litter the areas. To this extent, one often wonders whether there is any sense of human pain and morals in these areas.

But the Arab situation is not different from the African situation in that both originally derive from former Western imperialism. However, unlike in Africa, when Western rulers had left the Arab world, power fell in the hands of oil monarchs who have continued to use the oil wells to the disadvantage of the people.

On the other hand, the Arab situation presents different dimensions from the African experience, in that the Arab situation is sometimes fuelled by a presumed drive (dubbed divine call) to defend Islam especially from so-called Westernisation. As a result, much of the Arab world today, like Africa, has remained behind the rest of the world in human development, which explains the scenes that we often see in international media, in form of unending, and sometimes increasing, instabilities in the region. Nonetheless, the two situations converge in that both arise out of fundamental denials of human rights.

The significance of the book to the Arab situation.

In the Arab world, as in the African situation, people formerly suffered colonial imposition from the West. However, when the colonialists had left, neither region reversed the situation. Instead, the local elites took over the systems and turned them into their own. This is the reason we see instability and decline in these areas. The local rulers preside over heavily despotic systems, maintaining massive financial resources in foreign banks and enjoying exotic lifestyles in the local circumstances. As a result, the local people continue to decline in poverty and degeneration.

What needs to be done to correct the situation?

Any reader of the present book will have noticed that the appropriate solution to the Arab question, as the African one, is to review the contemporary state in the region. In the Arab, as in the African situation, there is need to open up the state with a view to free the people from repression and for participation, democracy and development. Only this would guarantee stability, development and sustainability in the region. Short of which, the region, as in Africa, is headed for a worse trouble.

BIBLIOGRAPHY

1. Abdullahi, Nasir M. Ahmed, "Human Rights Protection in Africa: Toward Effective Mechanism", _East African Journal of Peace and Human Rights_, Vol. 3, No. 1, 1997: 1-32.
2. African Commission on Human and Peoples' Rights (ACHPR), _Report of the African Commission's Work Group on Indigenous Populations/ Communities: Research and Information Visit to the Republic of Uganda, 14-17, 24-29, July 2006._
3. Akankwasa, R. R., "Human Rights Education and the Quest for Development: The Case of Uganda", _East African Journal of Peace and Human Rights_, Vol. 5, No. 2, 1999: 105-124.
4. Almond, Gabriel, A., & Coleman, James, S., _The Politics of The Developing Areas_, Princeton University Press, Princeton, New Jersey, 1971.
5. Ambrose P. Brendalyn, _Democratization and the Protection of Human Rights in Africa: Problems and Prospects_, Praeger Publishers, Westport, Connecticut, London, 1995: _http://www.questia. com/read/26239587?title=Democratization%20and%20 the%20Protection%20of%20Human%20Rights%20in%20 Africa%3a%20Problems%20and%20Prospects_

6. Amin, Shamir, *Maldevelopment: Anatomy of a Global Failure*, The United Nations University/ Third World Forum - Studies in African Political Economy, United Nations University Press, Tokyo, 1990.

7. Beardshaw and Palfreman, *The Organization in its Environment*, 4th Ed., Pitman Publishing, London, 1993.

8. Benedek Wolfgang and Nikolova Minna, *Understanding Human Rights: Manual on Human Rights Education*, Human Security Network, Graz, Austria, 2003.

9. Brett E. A., *Colonialism and Underdevelopment in East Africa: The Politics of Economic Change 1919-1939*, Heinemann, London, 1981.

10. Burkey Stan, *People First: A Guide to Self-Reliant, Participatory Rural Development*, Zed Books Ltd., London, 1993.

11. Conde H. Victor, *A Handbook of International Human Rights Terminology*, 2nd Ed., University of Nebraska Press, Lincoln and London, 2004.

12. Cornforth Maurice, "Materialism and the Dialectical Method", *Dialectical Materialism: An Introduction*, Vol. 1, Lawrence & Wishart, London, 1987.

13. Dag Hammarskjöld Foundation, *The State and the Crisis in Africa: In Search of a Second Liberation*, Uppsala, Sweden, 1992.

14. *Daily Monitor* (Uganda), Tuesday, February 5, 2008.

15. *Daily Monitor* (Uganda), Friday, December 16, 2011.

16. *Daily Monitor* (Uganda), Tuesday, February 26, 2013.

17. Donnelly, Jack, "What are Human Rights?" in Clack et al (Editors), *Introduction to Human Rights*: http://usinfo.state.gov

18. Gingyera-Pinycwa, A. G. G., "Refugees and Internally Displaced People in Africa on the Eve of the 21st

Century", *East African Journal of Peace and Human Rights*, Vol. 5, No. 1, 1998: 45-52.

19. Gutto, B. O. Shadrak, "The Rule of Law, Democracy and Human Rights: Whither Africa?", *East African Journal of Peace and Human Rights*, Vol. 3, No. 1, 1997: 130-139.

20. Harrison, Paul, *The Greening of Africa: Breaking Through in the Battle for Land and Food*, International Institute for Environment and Development-Earthscan, Paladin Grafton Books, London, 1989.

21. http://en.wikipedia.org/wiki/Ideological

22. http://en.wikipedia.org/wiki/Purchasing_power_parity

23. http://en.wikipedia.org/wiki/Southern_Sudan

24. http://en.wikipedia.org/wiki/Technological_development

25. http://jubileeresearch.org/databank/africamap.htm

26. http://www.economywatch.com/economic-statistics/country/Uganda

27. http://www.imf.org/external/np/exr/facts/hipc.htm

28. http://www.jubileeresearch.org/databank/profiles/uganda.pdf

29. http://www2.ohchr.org/english/law/progress.htm

30. http://www.udn.or.ug/pub/external%20debt%20.pdf

31. http://www.unfpa.org/rights/principles.htmhttp://youthink.worldbank.org/issues/development/

32. http://youthink.worldbank.org/4kids/development/developmentstory1.php

33. Hyden, Goran, *No Shot-Cuts to Progress: African Development Management in Practice*, Heinemann Educational Books Ltd, London, 1983.

34. Ingham Kenneth, *A History of East Africa*, Longmans, London, 1962.

35. Kabwegyere, B. Tarsis, *The Politics of State Formation: The Nature and Effects of Colonialism in Uganda*, East Africa Literature Bureau, Nairobi, 1974.

36. Lamwaka, H. Caroline Clara, 'Civil war and the peace process in Uganda, 1986-1997', *East African Journal of Peace and Human Rights*, Vol. 4, No. 2, 1998: 139-169.

37. Lomo, A. Zachary, "The Struggle for Protection of the Rights of Refugees and IDPs in Africa: Making the Existing International Legal Regime Work", *Berkeley Journal of International Law*, Vol. 18, No. 2, Boalt Hall School of Law, University of California, Berkeley, 2000: 268-284.

38. Maddex L. Robert, *International Encyclopaedia of Human Rights: Freedom, Abuses, and Remedies*, CQ Press, Washington, D.C., 2000.

39. Mazrui, A. Ali (Prof), "Decaying Parts of Africa Need Benign Colonisation", *a* reproduction in *CODESRIA Bulletin*, Number 2, 1995.

40. Museveni, K. Yoweri, *What is Africa's Problem?*, NRM Publications, Kampala, 1992.

41. Nabuguzi Emmanuel, "Ethnic Conflict and the Democratic Question in Uganda", *Journal of Behavioural and Social Sciences*, Vol. 1994, No. 3: *Special Issue: Nation Building and Sub-Cultures*, pp.111-130.

42. Norwegian Agency for Development Cooperation (NORAD), *Evaluation of The Norwegian Development Cooperation Through Norwegian Non-Governmental Organisations in Northern Uganda 2003-2007: Evaluation Report 3/2009.*

43. Nzita Richard and Mbaga-Niwampa, *Peoples and Cultures of Uganda*, Fountain Publishers Ltd, Kampala, 1995.

44. "Obama Ghana Speech: Full Text" at: http://www.huffingtonpost.com/2009/07/11/obama-ghana-speech-full-t_n_230009.html

45. Perham M., and Simmons J., *African Discovery: An Anthology of Exploration*, Faber and Faber, London, 1961.

46. Rosenberg Nathan and Birdzell L. E. Jr., *How the West Grew Rich: The Economic Transformational of the Industrial World*, Popular Prakashan, Bombay, 1987.

47. *Rtd. Col. Dr. Kizza Besigye vs. Electoral Commission & Yoweri Museveni - Supreme Court of Uganda Presidential Election Petition No. 01 of 2001 [Kampala Law Reports (KALR) 2001].*

48. *Rtd. Col. Dr. Kizza Besigye vs. Electoral Commission & Yoweri Museveni - Supreme Court of Uganda Presidential Election Petition No. 01 of 2006.*

49. *Ten Point Programme of NRM*, NRM Publications, 1986.

50. *The Sunrise* (Uganda), January 11-18, 2008.

51. The World Bank, *Sub-Saharan Africa: From Crisis to Sustainable Growth - A Long-Term Perspective Study*, Washington, D.C., 1993.

52. United Nations Declaration on the Right to Development.

53. United Nations Declaration on Social Progress and Development.

54. United Nations Humanitarian Coordination Unit (UNHCU), *Humanitarian Update Uganda*, Vol. 2, Issue 9, 27 November 2000.

55. United Nations Office of the High Commissioner for Human Rights (UNOHCHR), *Human Rights: A Compilation of International Instruments*, Vol. 1 (First

Part), Universal Instruments, United Nations, New York & and Geneva, 2002.

56. Wairama, G. Baker, *Uganda: The Marginalization of Minorities*, Minority Rights Group International, 2001.

57. Walubiri, Moses, "Tribalism and the Tragic Tale of Africa's Stolen Elections", *The Sunrise* (Uganda), January 11-18, 2008.

58. Wangoola, Paul, *Miijo: On "The African Crisis" Peoples Popular Participation and the Indigenous NGO in Africa's "Recovery" and Development*, African Association For Literacy and Adult Education (AALAE), Nairobi, 1991.

59. Wanyande, Peter, *Themes in World History*, Book Two, Longman Secondary History, Longman Kenya, 1991.

www.ingramcontent.com/pod-product-compliance
Lightning Source LLC
Chambersburg PA
CBHW050408290526
45786CB00003B/1179